English History

1000 Interesting Facts About England

Welcome Aboard, Check Out This Limited-Time Free Bonus!

Ahoy, reader! Welcome to the Ahoy Publications family, and thanks for snagging a copy of this book! Since you've chosen to join us on this journey, we'd like to offer you something special.

Check out the link below for a FREE e-book filled with delightful facts about American History.

But that's not all - you'll also have access to our exclusive email list with even more free e-books and insider knowledge. Well, what are ye waiting for? Visit the link below to join and set sail toward exciting adventures in American History.

To access your limited-time free bonus, go to: ahoypublications.com/

Introduction

*For centuries, the **history of England** has been tumultuous, filled with invasions, conquests, and revolutions.* **From the Anglo-Saxon invasion of 449 to present-day Brexit**, England's political landscape has been shaped by a variety of forces. This book will explore the major events and eras that have shaped **England's history**, from **the Norman Conquest** in 1066 **to the Reformation in 1517** and from **the Industrial Revolution** of the 18th century to **the Brexit vote** in 2016.

*You'll first learn about the **Anglo-Saxon invasion*** of 449 and its impact on England's political and social landscape. Then we will focus on the Norman Conquest of 1066 and its long-lasting effects on English culture.

*From there, you'll find fascinating facts about the reign **of William the Conqueror**,* including an in-depth look at how his rule changed England. We'll move on to some interesting facts about **the Plantagenet dynasty**, which ruled England beginning in 1154 and ended with **the Hundred Years' War** in 1453.

*And there were so many wars in **English history!*** We'll also explore **the Wars of the Roses**, a series of **civil wars** fought between two rival branches of **the Plantagenet dynasty**, and **the Reformation**, a period of religious upheaval that began in 1517.

*In the second section, we'll delve into **the Elizabethan era,*** **the English Civil War, the Restoration, and the Glorious Revolution**. You'll learn some interesting facts about the **Age of Enlightenment**, a period of intellectual and scientific progress that began in 1715.

*From there, **the Industrial Revolution** and the abolition of the slave trade will be discussed—you'll be surprised by the facts on those!* Afterward, we will look at **the Reform Acts, the Victorian era, the Crimean War, the Great Exhibition, the Irish Potato Famine, and the Boer Wars.**

Speaking of wars, you'll learn some interesting tidbits about the two world wars, **the welfare state, the Suez Crisis, decolonization, and the Thatcher years.** Finally, our last two chapters will cover **the Good Friday Agreement** and **Brexit**, respectively.

*By reading this book, you will gain an appreciation for how **England's history** has been shaped by a variety of forces over the past few centuries.* **From invasions to revolutions**, England's political landscape has been marked by tumultuous events and moments of progress. **You will surely find this book informative and intriguing**. We hope you'll continue your journey after finishing the book to learn more about **England's history!**

Table of Contents

Section 1: Exploring Pre-Modern England

Roman Britain

(43–c. 410 CE)

Explore the fascinating **history of Roman Britain**. This unique collection of facts will shed light on **the pivotal moments that shaped this captivating period.**
Though Roman forces under **Julius Caesar** landed in Britain, they did not stay long. The **Roman occupation began in 43 CE** when **Roman Emperor Claudius** initiated the invasion that would establish **Roman authority in Britain**. You'll read about **the rise of a new civilization in Britain** and the Romans' eventual withdrawal when Rome declined in power.

1. **Around 55 BCE, Julius Caesar** they were unsuccessful in establishing lasting Roman control.
2. **In 43 CE, Emperor Claudius ordered the Roman invasion of Britain**, which was led by **Aulus Plautius**. This marked **the official beginning of Roman rule**.
3. **Roman forces established the city of Londinium** (now London) **around 47 CE**, which became an important center of commerce and administration.
4. **Hadrian's Wall**, a fortification **built in 122 CE**, marked the northernmost boundary of **Roman Britain**, providing defense against northern tribes.
5. **The construction of the Antonine Wall began in 142**. It was located farther north in **modern-day Scotland**, but it was abandoned just a few decades later.

6. **Boudicca, queen of the Iceni tribe, led a major rebellion against Roman rule in 60 or 61**, resulting in the significant destruction of Roman settlements.
7. **Roman Britain experienced a period of relative peace and prosperity during the 2nd century CE, known as the Pax Romana.**

8. **By the 3rd century CE, Roman Britain had developed a thriving economy**, with trade networks and the production of various goods, including pottery and metalwork.

9. **Christianity began to spread in Roman Britain during the 3rd century**. By the 4th century, it had become the dominant religion.

10. **In 410, the Roman Empire withdrew its troops from Britain,** leaving the region vulnerable to raids by invading **Germanic tribes**.

11. **The departure of the Romans marked the beginning of the period known as sub-Roman Britain,** which was characterized by a decline in central authority.

12. **The legendary King Arthur**, often associated with **the period of sub-Roman Britain**, is believed by some to have led a **resistance against invading forces**.

13. **The Anglo-Saxon migration from continental Europe increased in the 5th and 6th centuries,** gradually replacing Roman-British culture.

14. **The Lindisfarne Gospels**, a remarkable illuminated manuscript, **was created around 700 CE,** showcasing **the blending of Celtic and Anglo-Saxon artistic traditions.**

15. **The legacy of Roman Britain can be seen today in the surviving archaeological sites,** Roman roads, and the influence of Latin on the English language.

Anglo-Saxon Invasion

(449–1066)

From 449 to 1066 CE, Britain was invaded by the Anglo-Saxons. The Anglo-Saxons were **Germanic tribes**. They were **mostly farmers and craftsmen**, but they were also **warriors** who fought **against the native Britons**, eventually dividing the land into several kingdoms, such **as Wessex, Essex, Sussex, and Mercia**. They were often at odds with each other. **"Britons" is the name for the people who lived in England before the Anglo-Saxon invasions.**

This era saw **great artistic achievements**, including literature like **Beowulf** and the **Anglo-Saxon Chronicle**, and advancements in **metalworking** skills and **architecture**. In 1066, these advances were halted when **the Anglo-Saxons were defeated by the Normans**, leading to significant changes politically, economically, and socially.

16. **The Anglo-Saxons began migrating to England around 449**. The Anglo-Saxons shortly became the dominant force in England. **They ruled until 1066**.

17. **Three Germanic tribes made their way to England: the Angles, Saxons, and Jutes**.

18. **They were collectively called the Anglo-Saxons.** They were the first people to be called **"English."**

19. **They came from northern Europe to England** in search of new land from their original homes in what is today **northern Germany and Denmark**. These places were too crowded. Too many tribes lived in the areas around their homelands.

20. **Though the Jutes, a Germanic tribe from Denmark, joined the Angles and Saxons migrating to England**, it is believed they were assimilated into Anglo-Saxon culture about a century after their arrival.

21. **The Anglo-Saxon invasion changed England forever**. They brought their language (which became Old English), customs, beliefs, and laws.

22. Important figures who lived during this era include **Alfred the Great**, who defended **England against Viking invasions**; **Bede, a monk** and **scholar; Offa of Mercia**, regarded as one of the most powerful kings in England during his time; **and Ethelbert of Kent**, who became **the first Anglo-Saxon king to convert to Christianity**.

23. One famous battle during this time was the **Battle of Edington (878),** in which King **Alfred the Great of Wessex** defeated a large Viking army.

24. **Danish and Norwegian Vikings began raiding along British** coastlines from the 8th century onward.

25. **The Anglo-Saxon tribes were divided into seven small kingdoms known as the Heptarchy**. These kingdoms were independent of each other. They often fought one another.

26. Eventually, **the Kingdom of Wessex became the most powerful**. It unified all seven into one large kingdom known as **England or the "Land of the Angles."**

27. **Strong kings had control over laws, taxes, military matters, and government decisions.** They were responsible for the people's welfare. However, kings often sought advice from their ealdormen, a type of governor.

28. **Wergild ("man price") determined how much compensation a person** should receive if they were wronged or injured or if a family member was killed.

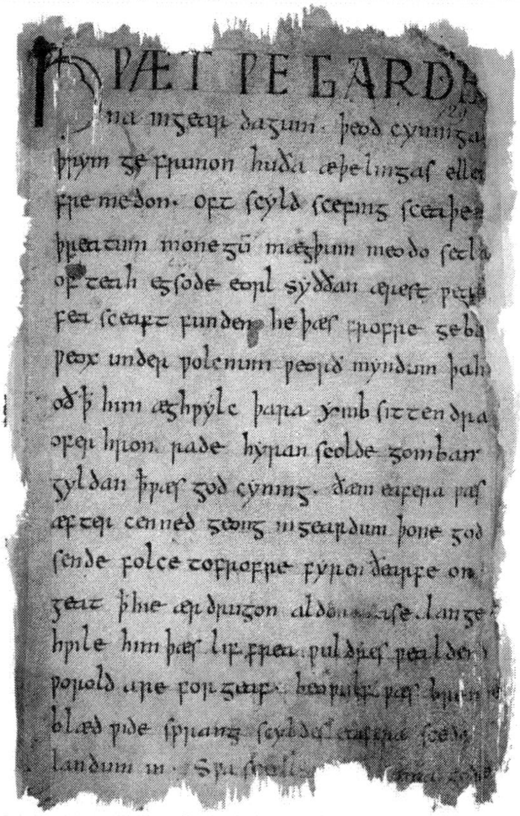

29. **Important literary works from this era include *Beowulf*** (a heroic epic poem) and **Bede's *Ecclesiastical History of the English People*** (an important sourcebook about early Christianity in Britain). **The *Anglo-Saxon Chronicle***, a record of events that took place during the reign of **Alfred the Great** (r. 871-899), is one of the most important Anglo-Saxon references.

30. The later **Anglo-Saxon period saw an increase in literacy and education**. Schools were established to teach **Latin and Greek literature**, **mathematics**, and **philosophy** to the upper class.

31. **The Anglo-Saxons originally believed in the many Germanic gods**, like **Woden/Odin** (the father of the gods), **Thunor/Thor** (the god of thunder), **Freya** (the goddess of love), and **Tiw/Tyr** (the god of war). All of these gods were venerated by the Anglo-Saxons' later enemies, the Vikings.

32. **Their beliefs changed once Christianity started to spread**. The religion was first introduced by **St Augustine of Canterbury in 597 when Pope Gregory** I sent him on a mission to convert the Anglo-Saxons.

33. **The Anglo-Saxons were very skilled craftsmen**. They worked with wood, stone, metal, leather, and textiles to create beautiful works of art and practical items, such as **weapons and tools.**

34. **Anglo-Saxon architecture was characterized by timber buildings** with thatched roofs. Later periods saw the introduction of more lasting materials like **brick and stone**.

35. **Homes during this era varied depending on social class**. Kings and nobles lived in fancy halls, but most people lived in very simple huts and cottages.

36. **The Anglo-Saxon period saw the construction of burghs**, fortified towns. Any British town with "burgh" at the end was founded during this time.

37. **Their most important form of entertainment was storytelling**, which would often include elements of mythology and heroic deeds.

38. **Pre-Christian Anglo-Saxons believed in a variety of magical creatures**, including elves, dragons, fairies, and giants, which were often mentioned in stories from this era.

39. **Music was popular among all classes**. Instruments included drums, flutes/pipes, harps, and lyres. Music styles ranged **from folk songs to epic poems** set to primitive melodies.

40. **Games were also played**. **Dice games like knucklebones**, which was similar to modern-day jacks, were popular.

41. **Drinking alcohol was common**. Mead, a beverage made with honey, and ale, a **beer made from barley,** were very popular. **Alcoholic drinks were often drunk instead of water**. Water often carried bacteria, which made people sick.

42. **Traditional clothing at this time consisted mostly of woolen garments for men and women.** They wore **tunics** (long shirts), **cloaks or coats**, or **trousers or hose**. Women wore linen shifts, usually a long shirt tied at the waist. **Wealthy women wore dresses**. Almost everyone wore leather shoes or boots.

43. **The average lifespan in Anglo-Saxon England was less than forty years** for most people. Royalty, especially kings, tended to live a bit longer.

44. **By the end of the Anglo-Saxon period, England was a very wealthy nation**. Foreign rulers sought to control it, such as the Normans and the Vikings.

45. **The Anglo-Saxon period ended in 1066 when William of Normandy, later known as William the Conqueror, invaded England**.

Vikings in England

(793–1066)

The Vikings were people from Norway, Denmark, and Sweden who began to sail from their Scandinavian homes to explore and raid the world around them in the 8th century CE. Most Swedish Vikings traveled east to Russia and Ukraine, but **the Danes and Norwegians traveled west**. Initially, **they raided England** for riches but later came to settle.

Over the years, **the Vikings and the English fought many battles**. At one point, **the Scandinavians controlled much of England. Their chief city was Jorvik**, today's York, in northeastern England. The area around the city and across the country to the Irish Sea was called the **Danelaw** by the Anglo-Saxons. Learn more about this adventurous and dangerous time with these thirty facts!

46. **Vikings raided, traded, and then settled in many parts of Britain and Ireland.**

47. **In the 800s, many Vikings and their families began to settle in England**, especially in the north and the southeastern part of the country known as **East Anglia**.

48. **Most of the Vikings who settled in the northeastern part of England were Danes. Norwegian Vikings, called the Norse**, settled in the northwest part of England and the southwest part of Scotland, along with the northern Orkney and Hebrides islands. **Vikings also established bases and cities in Ireland.**

49. **Though the Vikings controlled islands off the coast of Scotland** and some towns in the English/Scottish border regions, **they never controlled Scotland like they did parts of England.**

50. **When battles between the Vikings and Anglo-Saxons began**, the Vikings had an advantage. Many Vikings had been in battle before. Many of the early **Anglo-Saxon armies they met were largely made up of the *fyrd*** (pronounced similar to "feared"), who were **farmers and peasants** ordered to serve in the army. **Most of them had no training or experience.**

51. **No place was safe from Viking raiders, as their ships were capable of traveling even shallow rivers.**

52. **Monasteries were the prime targets of Viking raids in the initial Viking period.** These buildings were often very rich in gold coins and religious items.

53. **The most famous raid of a monastery was the first raid on the island of Lindisfarne** on the northern coast of England in 793.

54. **As the interaction between the Anglo-Saxons and Vikings grew**, so did **the spread of Christian beliefs among the Vikings.**

55. **Contrary to what many people believe, the Vikings and English often lived in the same areas.** They traded with one another and occasionally intermarried.

56. **The Vikings didn't bring death and destruction to England**. Because many Vikings established trading networks, England began to trade with many more cultures.

57. **Many archaeological finds in England from this period** came from as far away as the Middle East, Russia, and Ukraine, places where the Vikings had settled or had trading stations.

58. **Viking art in the form of woodwork and jewelry was very similar to pre-Christian Anglo-Saxon artwork**. This is not surprising since some **Vikings came from the same areas as the Angles, Saxons, and Jutes** before they traveled to Britain.

59. **The modern city of York was known to the Vikings as Jorvik.** It was the most important Viking city and fortress in England.

60. **Control of York ("Jorvik") went back and forth between the Vikings and Anglo-Saxons from about 850 to 954**, when the Anglo-Saxons took control of the city. Even under Viking King Canute, York was governed by the Anglo-Saxons.

61. **Today, it's easy to identify towns in England that were founded by the Vikings**. For example, towns and cities that end in "by" were founded by the Danes.

62. **Though the land in England controlled by the Vikings grew, shrank, and moved over time,** the northeastern and north-central **part of England became known as the Danelaw**, the area where the law of the Danes was in effect.

63. **The area of England north of Liverpool and into the famous Lake Country was controlled by Norwegian Vikings** during the Viking period rather than the Danes.

64. **The Great Heathen Army, also known as the Great Viking Army, invaded England in 865.** Before this, most Viking invasions of England were smaller raids.

65. **Legend has it that the legendary Viking Ragnar Lothbrok's three sons led the Great Heathen Army.** Historians aren't sure if Ragnar was a legend or a real person.

66. **One of the men who claimed to be Ragnar's son was Ivar the Boneless.** Some historians and archaeologists believe **that Ivar was killed in a battle near Repton**, where a mass grave with Viking bodies was found in the early 1970s.

67. **One of the ways we study Viking history is by finding and studying the many hoards of coins, jewelry, weapons, and precious metals the Vikings buried underground.** Hoards are still being found in England and other places to this day.

68. **By the mid-9th century, the Vikings controlled much of England.** The only Anglo-Saxon kingdom left was Wessex.

69. **For fifteen years, the king of Wessex, later known as Alfred the Great, united the Saxon kingdoms, fought the Vikings**, and pushed them away from the borders of his kingdom.

70. **In 1002, the king of Wessex, Æthelred (eh-thel-red) the Unready, ordered a massacre of Danes in England.** Historians aren't sure how many Danes were killed in the **St. Brice's Day massacre.** Thousands could have been killed.

71. Although many people believe that **Æthelred's nickname means that he was unready, the title has its roots in the Saxon word *redeless*,** which means **"without counsel"** or "without advice."

72. **In 1016, Viking King Canute became king of England, Denmark, and Norway**. However, he named **the English Harold I** as his successor as king of England.

73. A famous **tale about King Canute** tells the story of how he **ordered the tides to stop coming in**. Many people today think this might be because he was crazy, but he did this to show his men that there were things he could not do.

74. **Before William of Normandy launched his invasion of England** in the fall of 1066, the last great Viking invasion of England took place in northeastern England. **Famous Viking warrior** (which means **"hard ruler"** in Old Norse) believed he had a claim to the English throne.

75. **Hardrada** was defeated and killed by **English King Harold Godwinson** at **the Battle of Stamford Bridge** on September 25th, 1066, just three weeks before **the Battle of Hastings.**

Norman Conquest

(1066–1075)

In this chapter, we'll explore **the Norman Conquest of England**. Let's look at the culture, language, laws, government, and architecture introduced **by William the Conqueror** and his sons. **The Norman Conquest** impacted **the economic and social structure of England.** There's so much to discover, so let's get started!

76. **The Norman Conquest was a very important event in English history**, taking place between 1066 and 1075.

77. **Prior to 1066, there weren't any large-scale battles fought between the English and armies from what is now France.**

78. **The Norman Conquest was a gradual process,** not just one single event.

79. **It started with the Battle of Hastings** on October 14th, 1066, when **Duke William of Normandy** (part of modern-day France) **invaded England**.

80. **William defeated King Harold II of England at the Battle of Hastings** and became the **first Norman king of England.**

81. Not long **before King Harold was defeated by William I,** his **Anglo-Saxon army fought and defeated the last great Viking army at the Battle of Stamford Bridge**. Many historians believe **Harold** might have won **Hastings** if **the Vikings had not invaded.**

82. **"Norman"** is a variation of the word **"Northmen." The Normans were originally Vikings who were given the land by the king of France** to protect the region from other Vikings.

83. **After winning the battle, William marched to London**, where **he was crowned king on Christmas Day in 1066 at Westminster Abbey by Archbishop Aldred of York.**

84. **William then established his court at Winchester Castle in Hampshire,** which became his main base for ruling England until his death in September 1087.

85. **Though William became king of England**, he spent most of the rest of his life in his homeland of **Normandy.**

86. **William I built many castles as a way of showing his strength to the people of England. Windsor Castle,** near **London**, was built during his reign.

87. **Many monasteries and abbeys were built in the years following the Norman Conquest.**

88. **The Normans are credited with introducing several buildings that were not previously seen in Britain, such as windmills, stone castles, and many Romanesque-style churches and cathedrals.** Some of them still stand today!

89. **The Normans spoke a French dialect,** which **became the language of the English court** until the 14th century.

90. **The Normans introduced some French elements to Old English**, which helped to evolve the English language we speak today.

91. **The new "Anglo-Norman" culture that developed in England after 1066 marked a new beginning in English history**. The people of England who united under the Norman kings can be recognized as the start of the modern-day **"English" culture**.

92. **Much Norman literature had to do with romance**. These romantic legends later influenced courtly culture in England, like **the famous stories of knights and damsels** in distress.

93. **The famous legend of Robin Hood is a story of the Anglo-Saxon resistance** to the Norman occupation of England.

94. **The Domesday Book, which was commissioned by William I,** is an important record that details life during this time. **The book includes information about landholdings, population numbers, and more.** The book was meant **to help William with taxation.**

95. **The most well-known piece of art about the Normans of England is the Bayeux Tapestry,** which tells the story of **the Norman Conquest**, including **the Battle of Hastings.**

96. **After the conquest, nobles who supported William became wealthy and powerful,** while those who opposed him had their lands taken away. Some even had to flee Britain!

97. During this period, **there were three main classes: the king and his family, nobles/lords/high clergy** (who owned most of the land), and the common people, most of whom did not own land.

98. **The Normans introduced feudalism into England**, meaning people worked for nobles in exchange for protection and the use of their land.

99. **Many of the new laws introduced by William were based on Roman law and French customs,** creating a hybrid system with elements from all cultures living in England at the time.

100. **William introduced a new form of punishment for rebellions called the Harrying**, which involved destroying villages or crops as retribution for crimes committed against him or his officials.

101. **Because William and his successors controlled Normandy in continental Europe, trade between England and Europe increased at this time.**

102. **Normans eventually established kingdoms in Sicily and the Holy Land**. This meant that at one time, **Normans ruled places from the North Sea to the Middle East.**

103. **William was very sick for five weeks before he died.** He died in September 1087, and his body was transported many miles to his **capital, Rouen, Normandy**. At the funeral, his abdomen exploded, covering the mourners with his insides. His body was quickly thrown into a hole and covered up.

104. In 1087, William's son, **William II, took control after his death**. William II ruled for a little over a decade before **Henry I** succeeded him. William II is also known as **William II Rufus** because of his flaming red hair. **"Rufus"** means **"red-haired"** in Latin.

105. **The Norman Conquest was the last time that England was invaded.** Though **Napoleon** and **Hitler** planned and prepared for their own **invasions of England**, they were defeated before these attacks could happen.

Plantagenet Dynasty
(1154–1485)

Now we will take a closer look at one of **the most famous English families and dynasties.** We'll discover thirty facts about how the Plantagenet family and its rule affected this period of England's history. You'll learn **interesting facts about how they established an empire**, reformed the legal system, and built universities.

106. **The Plantagenet dynasty ruled England from 1154 to 1485** and included many famous kings like **Henry II, Richard I** (the Lionheart), **John** (Lackland), and **Edward III.**

107. **"Plantagenet" comes from the Latin name *planta genista***, the yellow broom flower, which is the symbol of the ruling family of **the French province of Anjou**. The Plantagenets were originally from Anjou. The Plantagenet kings are often referred to as the Angevin kings of England. **An Angevin is someone from Anjou.**

108. One of the most powerful members of this dynasty was **Eleanor of Aquitaine**, who brought her vast lands in France with her when **she married Henry II in 1152**.

109. Before Eleanor married Henry II, **she had been the wife of King Louis VII of France**, but the marriage was annulled in 1152.

110. **While she was married to Louis, Eleanor actually joined the Christian armies on the Third Crusade and traveled to the Holy Land** to try to regain Christian control from the Muslims.

111. In 1173, **Henry II's son, called "Young Henry," revolted against his father. Eleanor was arrested and imprisoned for thirteen years** because she supported her stepson instead of her husband, whom she had grown to hate.

112. **Richard I, sometimes known as Richard the Lionheart** or Lionhearted, ruled from 1189 to 1199. **He fought against the Muslim ruler Saladin in the Third Crusade** and was one of the most influential figures of his time.

113. **King John ruled from 1199 to 1216. The Magna Carta was signed by King John** in 1215, **which limited his power to rule** without consulting a council of nobles first.

114. **Magna Carta means "great charter" in Latin** and is thought to have inspired the **US Constitution.**

115. **King John was forced to sign the Magna Carta after many English nobles vowed to revolt if he didn't**. Many nobles rebelled against John anyway in an attempt to reduce his power and replace his family on the throne.

116. **John's son, Henry III, became king, but he did have slightly less power** than English kings before John.

117. **King Edward I ruled from 1272 to 1307**. In 1290, **he issued a decree expelling all Jews from England.** They weren't allowed back into the country until 1656 under **Oliver Cromwell's** rule.

118. **During Edward I's reign, he enacted laws that punished those found guilty with death by hanging or drawing and quartering**, one of the cruelest forms of execution ever used.

119. In 1274, **Edward I ordered a census and a study of the government in various areas of England called the "Hundred Rolls."** A variety of legal reforms were introduced because of this study.

120. **Edward I added Wales to his realm** between 1277 and 1283. The Welsh still consider themselves the only remaining Britons.

121. During this period, **there were battles between England and Scotland** known as the Wars of **Scottish Independence**, which lasted for over thirty years in the late 13th and 14th centuries.

122. **The famous Scottish hero William Wallace fought King Edward I** at the beginning of the First Scottish War of Independence, which took place from 1296 to 1328.

123. **Edward III ruled from 1327 to 1377**. He created a special order of knights known as **the Knights of the Garter**, which still exists today.

124. In 1337, **King Edward III declared war on France**, which would later become known as **the Hundred Years' War**. It ended in 1453 when **Henry V signed the Treaty of Troyes**, giving up English claims over French lands.

125. **One famous Plantagenet king was Richard III,** who ruled from 1483 to 1485. **He was made famous in Shakespeare's play of the same name**, which was about **the famous Wars of the Roses** that you will read about shortly.

126. **Traveling minstrels or troubadours became popular during this period**. They often sang songs in the royal courts. Their songs were mostly about love or chivalry.

127. **Chivalry flourished among knights at tournaments during this time**. They proved their skill with weapons or jousted on horseback.

128. One of the most famous books in English history was **Thomas Malory's *Le Morte d'Arthur*** (*The Death of Arthur*). The book was written in the mid-15th century. It was the first comprehensive work on the stories of **the mythical King Arthur**.

129. One of the most important pieces of English literature written during this period was **Geoffrey Chaucer's *Canterbury Tales***, a collection of stories about pilgrims on their way to Canterbury Cathedral.

130. **During the Plantagenet dynasty, schools were founded all over England**. Some even taught Latin, Hebrew, and Greek. **These schools were not for everyone. Only the royals**, nobles, their families, and those destined for the clergy could attend.

131. **Oxford University, which is thought to have been founded in 1096 during Norman times,** became the largest university in England under the Plantagenets. The dynasty banned English students from studying in France. **Cambridge was founded in 1209 and was given a royal charter in 1231 by Henry III.**

132. **The number of fortified castles in England grew at this time.** The wars with the Scots, occasional rebellions, and the possibility of a French invasion caused the Plantagenets to fortify their realm.

133. **The Plantagenet dynasty saw an increase in trade with other countries in Europe,** which led to greater cultural exchange between England and its neighbors.

134. **The Plantagenets created a new system of taxation called lay subsidies**, which required people to pay taxes based on their income or assets. This system had rarely been used in Europe before this time.

135. **The English language continued to evolve during this era** due to the influence of the French after the Norman invasion and the rise of the Plantagenets.

The Hundred Years' War

(1337–1453)

The Hundred Years' War was fought between England and France. The war lasted from **1337 to 1453** and was a time of turmoil that had deep, lasting effects on England and its people. Let's look at thirty **captivating facts about the battles, weapons, and strategies** used on both sides. We will also discover how this very long war impacted both countries.

136. **The Hundred Years' War was a conflict between England and France** that lasted for 116 years.

137. **It began when King Edward III of England, who had a weak claim to the French throne,** invaded France in 1337, which led to a series of battles. The fighting did not end until 1453.

138. Many famous figures from both sides took part in this war, including **King Henry V** on the English side and **Joan of Arc, King Charles VII**, and **Bertrand du Guesclin** on the French side.

139. **It is estimated that over three million people were killed during the war**, making it one of **the deadliest conflicts in European history at that time**. Many of these deaths came from disease, which people contracted because of poor sanitation. The arrival of **the Black Death** from Asia also occurred during this period.

140. **The Black Death killed off a third of Europe's population** and drastically reduced the number of soldiers available for both sides in this prolonged war. **The pandemic might have been one of the factors that led to the war's eventual end.**

141. **The Battle of Auberoche in 1345 is considered one of Edward III's first major successes** during this conflict. His victory enabled him to capture many territories in southwestern France.

142. **In 1346, Edward III scored a decisive victory against Philip VI at Crécy** with his longbowmen, who defeated an army twice their size.

143. **In 1355, Edward III granted his son, Edward "the Black Prince," command over an army.** He used the army to raid French territories during what became known as the **Chevauchée**, meaning "promenade" or "horse charge." **The Black Prince** raided behind enemy lines on horseback.

144. **During this war, both sides used a variety of tactics**, such as siege warfare, mass use of the longbow by the English, ambush, and heavy cavalry charges.

145. **One key strategy used by both sides was to build huge castles as defensive fortifications** along their borders with each other. Many of them are ruins today.

146. **During this war, both sides used spies to gather information** on their enemy's tactics and plans. Some **historians believe that espionage played an important role** in determining who won certain battles!

147. In 1360, **the Treaty of Brétigny led to temporary peace between England and France**. The peace lasted until 1369, when hostilities resumed after **Charles V rejected its terms**.

148. **The Battle of Agincourt** in 1415 saw the English, led by **Henry V,** emerge victorious, even though the enemy outnumbered them six to one.

149. One key moment during the war was when **Henry V captured Harfleur** (1415) on his way to **the Battle of Agincourt**. This was a major victory for the English, and it gave them access to a much-needed port.

150. **The English first used cannons at the siege of Harfleur**, which helped them knock down some of the city's defenses.

151. **During the Hundred Years' War, the English forces managed to capture large parts of France, including Normandy, Aquitaine, and Poitou**. However, they eventually lost control over these territories by 1453 when peace was agreed upon.

152. In 1394, **John Hawkwood, one of the most famous commanders in English history, managed to break through French defenses at Meaux** using innovative siege tactics, such as mining and counter-mining tunnels beneath walls.

153. **Joan of Arc, known as the "Maid of Orléans,"** was a teenage peasant girl who led an army against the English in 1429 after hearing voices from God telling her to do so. **She correctly proclaimed victories before they happened.** People believed she had a personal connection with God.

154. **One reason England ultimately lost was that Charles VII reunited a very divided France under his rule**, giving him a huge advantage in terms of resources.

155. **This long-running conflict had a huge economic impact on Europe** at that time, draining resources and disrupting trade routes, which caused food shortages across Europe.

156. **One key battle from the later stages of this conflict was fought at Formigny in 1450.** French forces under Jean de Villiers defeated an army led by Thomas Kyriell.

157. **De Villiers combined new tactics, like cannon fire, with traditional strategies**, like cavalry charges. This battle marked a turning point in the war. **France would eventually win in 1453.**

158. **Toward the end of the war, the English were suffering from heavy losses and difficulty in supplying their troops across the English Channel**. Disease also took its toll.

159. **The last battle of the Hundred Years' War was fought at Castillon (1453).** This ended with **a decisive French victory** which effectively marked the end of the English claim on the French throne.

160. **This conflict also saw the first use of guns on European battlefields**, although these firearms were much less effective than traditional medieval weaponry like swords and arrows.

161. **The Hundred Years' War led to the creation of new technologies, such as improved crossbows,** which could fire more powerful arrows at longer distances. **Crossbows helped both sides gain an advantage** over each other during certain battles.

162. **This war marked a transition from traditional medieval warfare toward modern tactics,** which included standing armies, better use of **artillery weapons** (like cannons) combined with infantry forces, and siege engines.

163. **The Hundred Years' War marked the dawn of the age of chivalry**. **Knights** began using **armored horses wearing** full plate armor. **Soldiers** were no longer just mounted archers or light cavalrymen. **"Chivalry"** is an English word with French roots. ***Cheval* is French for "horse."**

164. **Tales of chivalry became quite popular at this time.** People loved to read stories about mounted knights fighting one another and courtly love **between knights and "damsels in distress."**

165. **This long and bloody war was a major cultural event in European history**, with many contemporary writers and poets writing about it in their works.

Wars of the Roses

(1455–1487)

This chapter will explore the fascinating history of **the Wars of the Roses, a civil war in England** that lasted from 1455 to 1487. **It was fought between two branches of the royal house of Plantagenet.** We'll take a look at thirty interesting facts about the people, battles, politics, and legacy of this major turning point in English history.

166. **The Wars of the Roses was a civil war in England** that was fought between 1455 and 1487.

167. **England has had more than one civil war, although there is only one conflict called *the* English Civil War.** That war took place between 1642 and 1652. We'll tell you more about that war in another section.

168. **The war was fought between two branches of the House of Plantagenet,** known as **the House of Lancaster** (symbolized by a red rose) and the **House of York** (symbolized by a white rose).

169. **These wars had an impact on fashion, with people wearing their house colors to show support.** They wore red or white roses at events like tournaments or festivals, which were popular during this time.

170. **These two sides fought for control over England until Henry Tudor of Lancaster won the Battle of Bosworth Field in 1485**, where he defeated Richard III of York.

171. **During these wars, many powerful families supported either side, such as the Nevilles, Percys, Stanleys, Greys, and Talbots**. They all fought for control over England's throne.

172. **Many famous people were involved in the Wars of the Roses**, like **Margaret Beaufort**, who helped her son, **Henry Tudor**, gain power through alliances with other noble families. **John Neville** acted as commander-in-chief for his brother, known as **Warwick the Kingmaker.**

173. **The Battle of Towton in 1461** is considered to be one of **the bloodiest battles ever fought on English soil**. No one knows for sure, but it is said that an estimated twenty-eight thousand people were killed during the battle, which took place in a heavy snowstorm.

174. **Edward IV won many battles for York during these wars**, allowing him to **become king in 1461**. He ruled for twelve years, although he had to flee the country for a short period of time.

175. **Richard III is remembered as a tyrant king because he usurped power from Edward V, Edward IV's son.**

176. **Richard was also thought to have kidnapped and killed the young princes,** his nephews, to prevent them from claiming the throne.

177. **Richard III was later immortalized by William Shakespeare as an evil tyrant in his play *Richard III*,** which helped shape people's opinions of him. Today, historians believe he might not have been as bad as originally thought.

178. **Richard was the last English king to die in battle**, doing so at Bosworth Field, the final battle of **the Wars of the Roses**.

179. **Richard III's body was found in 2012 in the Grey Friars site in Leicester County in an open area** that once was a car park. In 2015, **Richard III was given a royal burial in Leicester Cathedral.**

180. **Margaret Beaufort played an important role in bringing about peace between both sides through her marriage negotiations with Lord Stanley**, who then helped her son **Henry Tudor** obtain victory at **Bosworth Field** against **Richard III.**

181. Women played an important role during this period, like **Elizabeth Woodville**, the non-noble wife of **Edward IV,** whose unpopularity helped bring about **the Wars of the Roses. Margaret of Anjou, wife of Henry VI,** played a large role behind the scenes and was a key figure in the outbreak of the war.

182. **Margaret of Anjou** is another important female figure from this time period. She was **the queen consort of Henry VI** and a powerful leader in her own right, leading troops into battle at the Battle of Tewkesbury, where she was defeated by **Edward IV**.

183. **When the war ended, Henry VII married Elizabeth of York, daughter of Edward IV. Henry and Elizabeth were the parents of Henry VIII** and the grandparents of **Elizabeth I. Henry VII was the first Tudor monarch**, and **Elizabeth I was the last.**

184. At the end of the war, **the symbols of Lancaster and York were united into the Tudor Rose,** a rose with both white and red petals.

185. **One of the major reasons why these wars lasted so long was because both sides were evenly matched,** with neither side having a long-lasting clear advantage over the other until **Richard III's defeat at Bosworth Field**

186. **During this period, England also underwent many changes, including using more gunpowder weapons,** which made battles more destructive. New laws were created, and taxes were increased because the military campaigns took up so many resources.

187. **These wars had a major impact on English politics, with nobles becoming less powerful while Parliament began playing a slightly larger role in national decisions**.

188. **Many towns that were destroyed during this conflict never fully recovered**, leading to lasting economic decline in some areas. It also caused mistrust between different regions. Some of the regional rivalries in soccer, for instance, date back to **the Wars of the Roses.**

189. **This conflict caused much suffering throughout England, with people fleeing their homes or being killed due to battles taking place nearby**. Famine, disease, and poverty spread across many regions, making life difficult for those who survived.

190. **It has been estimated that up to 100,000 men were killed during the Wars of the Roses,** making it one of the bloodiest conflicts ever fought on British soil.

191. **The Wars of the Roses had an impact on literature,** with writers like **William Shakespeare** writing about it in their works. To this day, **the Wars of the Roses** are a popular topic in historical novels.

192. **Music was also influenced by these wars**, with many songs written about it, such as **"Rose of England,"** which was very popular back in the day.

193. Despite everything that happened during these wars, **they ultimately helped to unify England. One king was recognized by everyone**, creating more stability and increasing trade between England and mainland Europe.

194. **The Wars of the Roses helped create a sense of national identity in England,** as people began to feel more connected and loyal toward their country.

195. **It has been over five hundred years since these wars ended**, but they are still remembered today at historical sites around Britain, such as **Bosworth Battlefield Heritage Centre** and **Richard III Visitor's Centre**, both located near **Leicester**.

The English Reformation

This chapter will explore **the momentous English Reformation**, a period of **religious and political revolution** that was affected by **the greater Protestant Reformation**. The Reformation **changed the course of history**; let's see how as we cruise through thirty interesting facts **about this important time in European history.**

196. **The Protestant Reformation was a religious and political movement that changed Europe in the 1500s**.

197. **It started when Martin Luther wrote his *Ninety-five Theses*,** criticizing the Catholic Church for its practices of selling indulgences and other corrupt activities.

198. **Luther was later excommunicated from the Catholic Church by Pope Leo X** in 1521, which officially began the Protestant Reformation throughout Europe.

199. **The Reformation led to the creation of many different forms of Protestantism, such as Calvinism, Lutheranism, and Anabaptists,** which later developed into denominations like **Baptists, Presbyterians, Methodists, and Congregationalists.**

200. **The English form of Protestantism is called Anglicanism**. In some places, it is referred to as Episcopalian.

201. **The Reformation had a huge influence on the English language since the Bible was translated into vernacular** (regional language). **Before, the Bible was printed in Latin.**

202. **William Tyndale was responsible for translating the Bible into English using the original Greek and Hebrew texts**. The first published edition came out in 1526, although revised versions were released posthumously **after Tyndale's execution**.

203. **Tyndale was executed in 1536** on charges of heresy. **He opposed Henry VIII's** annulment of Catherine of Aragon.

204. There were many influential theologians who interpreted the Bible differently. **John Calvin, Huldrych Zwingli, and Philip Melanchthon** are just some examples.

205. **In England, Thomas Cranmer helped Henry VIII with his infamous separation from Catherine of Aragon.** Henry VIII wanted a male heir, and Catherine had been unable to provide him with one. **Henry wanted to annul his marriage and marry a new wife, Anne Boleyn.**

206. **The pope refused to grant Henry a divorce since he didn't want to anger the Holy Roman emperor**. So, Henry decided to split from the Catholic Church, granting himself the separation he so greatly desired.

207. **King Henry VIII's Act of Supremacy was passed in 1534**. The act declared him the head of **the Church of England**. He no longer had to follow what the pope said.

208. **The pope was so upset by Henry's actions that he excommunicated the English king!**

209. **Henry's marriage to Anne Boleyn produced a child**, but he did not get the male heir that he wanted. **Anne Boleyn would eventually be executed on the grounds of treason.**

210. **Although Henry created a new church, he still kept many Catholic practices**.

211. **Though the archbishop of Canterbury ran the everyday business of the Church of England,** Henry VIII was ultimately in charge of the clergy and was considered "responsible" for the souls of his subjects.

212. **Church law, which had once rivaled the Crown's power**, was made subordinate to the laws of the country (aka the king).

213. **Henry VIII seized the land and riches of the Catholic monasteries and religious orders in England** to fund the new church and make himself richer.

214. **Thomas More, author of the classic book *Utopia*, was a government official and a staunch Catholic.** He was executed because he would not accept Henry VIII as the head of the Church of England. More is considered a saint by the Catholic Church.

215. **For at least two centuries after Henry VIII, Catholics in England were persecuted at times,** though the Stuart kings of England in the 17th century were Catholic.

216. **The Church of England changed more drastically during Edward VI's reign.** Edward VI was very young, so he relied on his advisors. These men desired more changes to the Church of England.

217. **In 1549, the Anglican Church introduced the *Book of Common Prayer*** in an effort to give further structure to the church and to unify its followers. A modern version of the book is still used in the Anglican Church today.

218. **Thomas Cranmer was largely responsible for the *Book of Common Prayer***, although he did borrow heavily from other sources.

219. **After Edward VI died, his sister, Mary, took the throne. Mary was a Catholic, and she wanted to reinstate the religion**.

220. **At first, Mary promoted tolerance, but she eventually began to crack down on Protestants.**

221. **Mary killed over three hundred people during her reign for not adhering to Catholicism.** One of those people was **Thomas Cranmer**.

222. **When Mary died, Elizabeth I took the throne. She reinstated the Church of England but took a more moderate approach**.

223. **In 1559, the Act of Uniformity was passed**, which authorized a revised version of the ***Book of Common Prayer.***

224. **As time passed, groups like the Puritans rose up**. They wanted to strip or "purify" the Church of England of any Roman Catholic practices.

225. **Though the English Reformation radically reduced the power of the Catholic Church in England,** the beliefs and rituals of the Church of England are similar to those of the Catholic Church in many ways.

Elizabethan Era

(1558–1603)

Immerse yourself in the intriguing history of **the Elizabethan era**. Uncover thirty interesting facts about **the culture and events of this period**. Explore the works of one of **the most influential writers in history: William Shakespeare**. Discover **how Queen Elizabeth I's reign impacted English society**, the English language, and science.

226. **The Elizabethan era** was a time when **the population of England and Wales grew** from three million to four million people.

227. **Most people lived in small villages made up of mostly wooden houses with straw roofs.** Some even lived in homes built into the ground. These homes were known as half-timbered houses.

228. **People ate very simple meals** consisting mainly of bread dipped in sauces, boiled eggs, and vegetables like carrots, onions, or cabbage cooked over an open hearth inside their house.

229. **No forks were used during meals**. Food was eaten with spoons or fingers. Knives were used to help cut food into smaller pieces.

230. **Young children didn't go to school** but were instead taught at home by their parents or tutors until around the age of seven. **Boys could attend grammar schools**, though most did not. **Most girls remained uneducated** unless they came from wealthy families who could afford teachers for them at home.

231. **There were no street lights**, so people carried oil lanterns while they walked around at night.

232. **Bathhouses were in England before Elizabeth's reign**. For a small price, people could cleanse themselves and socialize. **In the Elizabethan era, many bathhouses closed** because people began to believe that infection and disease could enter the body through scrubbed skin.

233. **People believed strongly in the power of herbs, plants, and stones as remedies for illnesses.** Leeches were also used to treat various forms of diseases, such as smallpox or scarlet fever. **Leeches were thought to suck out the "bad blood"** caused by these diseases.

234. **Due to poor sanitation and overcrowding in the cities, infectious diseases spread quickly through towns and villages**, resulting in outbreaks of the plague known as the **Great Pestilence**. Thousands died across England!

235. The same disease had afflicted Europe before in the 14th century. That name might sound more familiar; it was called **the Black Death.**

236. **People who practiced any religion other than Anglicanism were often punished because Elizabeth wanted to keep religious unity within her kingdom**. Her religious policies are known collectively as **the Elizabethan Religious Settlement**.

237. **Sir Francis Drake became one of the first English explorers to circumnavigate the globe in 1580** aboard his ship called the *Golden Hind* (a female deer).

238. **Explorers like Sir Walter Raleigh** went on expeditions to explore new lands and brought back exotic plants, animals, spices, and even tobacco to England.

239. **The Royal Navy was established by Elizabeth's father**, Henry VIII, in 1546. In 1588, the loosely organized navy defeated the more numerous Spanish Armada. **Spain wanted to land troops in England and put a Catholic on the English throne.**

240. **The most popular sport during this era was a game called bowls**, which involved rolling wooden balls toward a target on grass or dirt.

241. **People enjoyed watching theater performances**, which often included acrobatics, juggling, sword fighting tricks, and bull and bear baiting (where dogs were used to attack bulls and bears).

242. **Audiences for plays were often quite rowdy, yelling and making comments during the show.** Often, the audience near the stage stood and made up more of the common people. Rich or important people sat in the back or in primitive balconies to watch the show.

243. **Women were not allowed to be actors** but sometimes played the roles of male characters in plays by wearing masks and costumes. Young boys and younger men played female roles.

244. During this era, **William Shakespeare** wrote some of his most famous plays, such as ***Romeo and Juliet* and *Hamlet*.**

245. **Toward the end of Elizabeth's reign, Shakespeare and others built the famous Globe Theatre**, where many of Shakespeare's plays were performed. Today, you can visit a replica of the theater, which was erected in 1997.

246. **Music was an important part of life in Elizabethan England**. Musicians played **instruments like lutes and violins**. They also sang folk songs together.

247. During this period, **Elizabethan fashion was all about bright colors**, ruffles, and lace trimmings for both men's and women's clothing.

248. **Upper-class men often sported fanciful beards, while the women preferred to have long hair** curled up high or braided down low, with colorful ribbons and flowers woven throughout.

249. **Queen Elizabeth I had dozens of wigs made for her out of human hair or horsehair** so she could change styles frequently. Wigs also allowed her to hide her greying hair when she got older.

250. **Elizabeth's famous white makeup was lead-based**. Many historians believe that lead poisoning was a factor in Elizabeth's death.

251. **Elizabeth reputedly had tremendously bad breath**. She invented a paste that was thought to prevent breathing in "diseased air." It was supposed to smell good, but it was made of sugar and honey. **The paste likely rotted the queen's teeth**, which made her bad breath worse.

252. **In the first part of Elizabeth's reign, she was a much sought-after match.** Many kingdoms sent their princes to England to secure her hand in marriage. They knew England would be a powerful ally. **Elizabeth refused them all.**

253. **Queen Elizabeth I never married, but she did have favorites like Robert Dudley, who she referred to as "her sweet Robin."** There was also **Robert Devereux**, the Earl of Essex, who eventually rebelled against Elizabeth and was executed for treason.

254. One of Queen Elizabeth I's most famous quotes is, **"I know I have the body but of a weak and feeble woman; but I have the heart and stomach of a lion."**

255. **Elizabeth died without having children, making the question of her succession a very important and critical issue in her later life**. She never named a successor, but her chief minister, Robert Cecil, negotiated with **James VI of Scotland**, who had a claim to the throne since he was Elizabeth's cousin through Henry VI. **He became James I of England** in 1603.

The Age of Discovery
(1487–1800)

While England began to explore the world before **the Elizabethan era**, its **Age of Discovery didn't really hit its stride until Elizabeth's reign**. But don't worry; we have included facts about **England's earliest voyages**, as well as what happened during its peak of exploration.

These voyages played a crucial role in **expanding geographical knowledge**, establishing colonies, and shaping the course of history. From **John Cabot's exploration of North America to Captain James Cook's expeditions in the Pacific,** these voyages propelled England to the forefront of exploration, colonization, and maritime dominance.

256. **In 1497, Italian explorer John Cabot set sail on his first voyage to North America, sailing under the English flag**. He reached Newfoundland and became the first recorded European since the Vikings to explore mainland North America.

257. **In 1564, English pilot William Adams washed ashore in Japan** after the Dutch ship he was guiding was damaged in a storm. Japan had relations with Spain and Portugal already, but **Adams became the first Englishman in Japan**. His story was made famous in the novel and TV mini-series *Shogun*.

258. **Sir Francis Drake embarked on his famous journey in 1577**. He became the first Englishman to circumnavigate the globe, returning to England in 1580.

259. **In 1579, Drake landed on the Pacific coast of North America and claimed the area for England**, naming it Nova Albion (New Albion).

260. **In 1589, Drake embarked on what is known as the Drake-Norris Expedition**, which aimed to disrupt Spanish shipping and raid Spanish colonies in the Americas. This expedition was not successful.

261. **Sir Walter Raleigh sponsored the first English colony in the New World, known as Roanoke Colony,** in present-day North Carolina in 1585. However, the colony mysteriously disappeared, giving rise to the legend of **the "Lost Colony."**

262. **In 1607, the English established the colony of Jamestown in Virginia**. Jamestown became the first successful permanent English settlement in North America, **marking the beginning of English colonization** in the region.

263. **In 1609, Henry Hudson, an English explorer sailing for the Dutch**, embarked on an exploration of North America's northeastern coast, resulting in **the discovery of the Hudson River** and Hudson Bay.

264. **In 1610, Hudson, now sailing under the English flag, embarked on his final voyage in search of a Northwest Passage that people believed led to the Pacific Ocean**. Though he did not find the passage, the voyage laid the groundwork for subsequent English exploration in the area.

265. **In 1642, English explorer Abel Tasman**, sailing for the Dutch East India Company, **discovered Tasmania** and explored parts of present-day **Australia**, **New Zealand**, and other **Pacific islands**.

266. **The English established the Hudson's Bay Company in 1670**. This company played a significant role in the exploration and fur trade in **the Canadian Arctic region**.

267. **In 1768, Captain James Cook, an English explorer, embarked on his first voyage on the HMS *Endeavour***. This journey took him to **the Pacific**, where he made significant scientific and geographical discoveries.

268. **In 1772, Captain James Cook set out on his second voyage on the *Resolution*.** This expedition resulted in the discovery and mapping of various Pacific islands, including Easter Island.

269. **Captain James Cook died on February 14th, 1779**. He was killed in a violent encounter **with Hawaiian natives during his third voyage** of exploration in the Pacific. Cook and his crew had been attempting to resolve a tense situation with the local population when a fight broke out.

270. **In 1788, the English established the first permanent European settlement in Australia** with the arrival of **the First Fleet at Port Jackson** (Sydney). This marked the beginning of the colonization and development **of Australia as a British territory**.

The English Civil War
(1642–1651)

Now we'll explore **the English Civil War**. During this time, **the Royalists** (those supporting the monarchy) were pitted against **the Parliamentarians** (those who supported Parliament). The civil war involved important figures such as **Oliver Cromwell and Charles I. Learn** who fought on the side of **the Royalists** and the Parliamentarians' **New Model Army**.
For a time, **England had no king and was called the Commonwealth**. This war spurred significant political and **religious changes in England, Scotland, and Ireland**, like the adoption of **the English Bill of Rights** (similar to America's but over a hundred years older) and the rise of **the Puritans**.

271. **The English Civil War lasted from 1642 to 1651**. It was a conflict between supporters of **the monarchy (Royalists)** and supporters **of Parliament (Parliamentarians).**

272. **Parliament was the legislature of England** (and all of Great Britain today).

273. There were (and still are) two parts of Parliament: **the House of Commons**, made up of elected officials, and **the House of Lords**, made up of men (and now women) who came from the nobility.

274. **The House of Lords had much more power than it does today** and was banned by the Roundheads for a time after the war.

275. **Many Parliamentarians were concerned about King Charles I's** increasing movement to revitalize **the Catholic Church in England**.

276. **Oliver Cromwell, a leader of the Parliamentarians, was a key figure in the war**. He led England for a time after it ended as **"Lord Protector."**

277. **The Parliamentarians wanted to limit the king's powers**. They believed Parliament should have more power.

278. **Many leading Parliamentarians were Puritans**. The Puritans were a fundamentalist sect. **They believed everyone should read the Bible,** but they also believed their church elders were better equipped to interpret it. **Many Puritan groups grew to be less tolerant** of other Protestant belief systems.

279. **After the restoration of the monarchy, there was a crackdown on the Puritans**. They eventually fled to Holland and North America.

280. **The Royalists were led by King Charles I,** who many believed was Anglican in name only. **Charles was also married to a Catholic princess from France.**

281. **Many Protestants feared that he would restore Catholic influence**, though the war was mostly about **Charles trying to grab more power than the Parliamentarians** were comfortable with.

282. **The Royalists were commonly called Cavaliers**, a word that comes from the French word for **"cavalry" or "horse." The Parliamentarians were called Roundheads** due to their bowl-shaped haircuts.

283. **The Royalists were supported by most Irish people**, as Ireland remained a strongly Catholic part of Britain.

284. **The Scots supported both sides of the conflict**, with one powerful Scottish lord, **Lord Leven,** switching sides from the Crown to Parliament during the war.

285. **Welsh soldiers fought on both sides**, though no battles took place in Wales.

286. **Many Welshmen were Catholic and supported the king**, but many others supported Parliament, where they were also represented.

287. **The war was fought in many parts of England, Scotland, and Ireland**.

288. **The first battle of the English Civil War was the Battle of Edgehill in 1642.**

289. **Oliver Cromwell was one of the chief generals of the Roundheads** and led the New Model Army.

290. **The New Model Army** was made up of people who made the military their profession rather than the levies, or draftees, that had been used before.

291. Many of the leaders of **the New Model Army were nobles** with combat experience who brought their own private armies with them and merged them into **the larger Roundhead army.**

292. **King Charles I was said to have been quite brave**, but he was not a good military leader.

293. **The Roundheads were better organized and better equipped than the Cavaliers.**

294. **The Royalists had more money,** but **the Parliamentarians had a larger number of troops.**

295. **The Parliamentarians defeated the Royalists at the important Battle of Naseby in June 1645.** This battle was the turning point in **the English Civil War.**

296. About a month later, **the New Model Army destroyed the last effective Royalist fighting force** in **the Battle of Langport**.

297. **Charles was put on trial in London's Westminster Hall in January 1649**. This was the first time in history that a king was put on trial for crimes against his people.

298. **The Parliamentarians executed King Charles I for high treason in 1649,** though his supporters continued the war for another two years.

299. **Charles was the only English king in history to be executed.**

300. **At the beginning of the war, many Scottish nobles supported Parliament** instead of Charles because they sought more power for themselves. However, when he was executed, many turned against Parliament, but this ended in the defeat of the Royalist cause in 1651.

301. **The English Civil War, along with the later Glorious Revolution,** put an end to the absolute monarchy in England.

302. **Oliver Cromwell's military successes made him a powerful political figure in England.**

303. **Despite being a Parliamentarian during the war, Cromwell dissolved Parliament** in 1653 because of the many quarrels among the Parliamentarians. He ruled England as a virtual dictator from 1653 to 1658, when he passed away.

304. **Power struggles between different factions within Parliament and an ineffective government after the death of Cromwell** in 1658 **led to negotiations with the House of Stuart** and to the restoration of the monarchy in the form of **Charles II,** son of the executed king.

305. **Charles II had to promise not to restore Catholicism** as the national religion and follow laws that limited the power of the monarchy.

306. **Charles II had been king of Scotland for over ten years by the time he retook the English throne in 1660.**

307. **Both Charles I and II were members of the Stuart family**, a powerful Scottish clan with ties to the royal families in both England and Scotland.

308. From the beginning of **the Commonwealth** until **the Restoration** in 1660, **Great Britain was governed as a republic.**

309. **Though the Commonwealth had many flaws**, including putting too much power in the hands of the executive, this period was the first time Britain had ever been governed by anything other than a monarch.

310. **The changes that began after the death of Charles I** and during the Commonwealth resulted in **the English Bill of Rights in 1689**.

The Restoration

(1660–1688)

After the English Civil War, **the Restoration happened**. This period saw **the monarchy come back to England,** although it was more limited than before. Let's look at thirty interesting facts about England's culture during this era, including **the scientific discoveries of Isaac Newton.**

311. **The Restoration was a period of time in British history from 1660 to 1688**. The name of the period comes from **King Charles II** being restored to the English throne after the end of the English Civil War.

312. **The Age of Reason** began during this period. Many scientific discoveries based on logic, evidence, and the new **scientific method** replaced guesswork, superstition, and religious belief as the basis of scientific research.

313. **Isaac Newton, Robert Boyle, Edmond Halley**, and many others made important contributions to many fields of science at this time.

314. **The Restoration** was a time of growing religious tolerance and freedom of speech.

315. The period saw **the rise of coffee houses, playhouses**, and **newspapers**.

316. **The first English newspapers were published during this period.**

317. The first women's magazine, called **"The Ladies Mercury,"** was published in 1693.

318. The period saw a flowering of the arts, with writers such as **John Dryden and William Congreve** penning works.

319. **John Locke** was one of the foremost writers of the time. Although he lived before the period historians call **the Enlightenment**, he is often considered one of the first "enlightened" writers because of his call for **individual liberty** and **democratic ideals**.

320. **When Charles II** came to the throne, he had **Oliver Cromwell's** body dug up and hung for everyone to see. Cromwell had been instrumental in the sentence and execution of **Charles II's** father, **Charles I.**

321. **The Bank of England was established** in 1694. It was the first real attempt to centralize power over the economy and provide unified rules about currency, interest, and more.

322. **The population of England and Wales doubled during this period.**

323. **The slave trade began to expand during the Restoration.**

324. **The East India Company** was founded in 1600 and began trading with India. During the Restoration, it expanded its reach in India.

325. **The Navigation Acts were passed** in 1651, 1660, and 1663. These acts imposed trade restrictions on the English colonies in America.

326. **The Whigs and Tories were two political parties** that developed during this period. Generally speaking, **Whigs** tended to oppose the monarchy, and **Tories** tended to support it.

327. **The Restoration** gave its name to a whole genre of drama and comedy, with styles starting to shift away from the "looser" language and style of **Shakespeare** toward a more formal and structured writing style.

328. **The Royal Society was established** in 1660 and was dedicated to promoting scientific research.

329. **The Great Fire of London** in 1666 destroyed much of the city.

330. **Charles II** and his close friends, who had spent time in France during the Commonwealth period, valued French clothing, writing, and drama. In Charles II's court, a more **"French" style**, which was much more formalized than what the English were used to, became popular.

331. **The first police forces were established in Scotland and England** in the 1600s, though these were far different than the police as we know them today.

332. Many critics of **the Stuart court** saw it as decadent, meaning that the king and his followers enjoyed a little too much wine, women, and song. They were more concerned with their own pleasures than ruling the country.

333. **In 1685, James II took the throne**. He was Charles II's younger brother.

334. At first, **James had widespread support** from people in England, Ireland, and Scotland.

335. As time passed, people became dissatisfied with his rule. **James II was interested in restoring the Catholic Church** to its former position within England. The people did not want Catholicism to be forced on them.

336. **When he gave birth to a son, the people were worried that he would begin a Catholic dynasty.** They revolted against his rule.

337. **The Glorious Revolution of 1688 saw the overthrow of King James II** and the establishment of a constitutional monarchy.

338. **The Glorious Revolution** inspired later acts. For instance, **the Act of Toleration** in 1689 granted freedom of worship to **Protestant Nonconformists**. Nonconformists were Protestants that had different beliefs than the predominant Church of England.

339. **The Act of Union in 1707** established the United Kingdom. **This act "united" Scotland and England.** Queen Anne, James II's daughter, was on the throne at this time.

340. **Ireland had been invaded by the English** in the 1500s and would become part of **the United Kingdom** in 1801.

The Glorious Revolution

(1688–1689)

And now we have the remarkable events of **the Glorious Revolution**, which happened between 1688 and 1689. Here are thirty interesting facts about this **revolutionary period,** including its **causes and consequences**. We'll discover **how the power of the monarchy was limited** and how a strong, **unified nation was established**. Furthermore, we will learn how **the Glorious Revolution** helped to spread the ideas of limited government throughout Europe.

341. **The Glorious Revolution** was a peaceful event in which **Catholic King James II** of England was **replaced by William III and Mary II**, who were **Protestant rulers**.

342. **The Glorious Revolution** is also known as **the Bloodless Revolution** because no fighting between armies took place.

343. Although most accounts describe **the Glorious Revolution** as **peaceful with little bloodshed,** some historians argue there were still casualties due to riots or revenge attacks. It's estimated that around **five thousand people died** in the months leading up to this event.

344. **England had experienced religious turmoil under King James II, who tried to bring back Catholicism as the official religion**. His reign ended when he fled to France after losing support from most nobles and clergymen.

345. **Queen Mary II was the daughter of James II** and **his first wife**. She was also **the niece of Charles II.**

346. **William III was Mary's husband**. He arrived **from Holland to take over the English throne** in 1688 with fifteen thousand soldiers at his side.

347. One important figure during **the Glorious Revolution** was **John Locke**. He wrote about **natural rights** like life, liberty, health, and property. His ideas were influential in the making of **the Bill of Rights** and also influenced **the American Revolution**.

348. Another important figure during **the Glorious Revolution** was **John Churchill**, later known as **Duke of Marlborough**. Churchill defeated forces loyal to James II at battles like **the Battle of Sedgemoor** and **the Battle of Dunkeld**, which helped **secure victory for Protestants in England.** He later defeated the armies of **Louis XIV at Blenheim**. **John Churchill was Winston Churchill's 6x-great-grandfather.**

349. This event saw many **Protestants from different backgrounds come together** to support the cause **against James II's rule.**

350. **The Glorious Revolution** saw the rise of **the Whig Party in England**, which was a **political party that supported Protestantism** and limited government power.

351. **After James II fled England**, his supporters (known as **Jacobites**) tried several times to put him back on the throne. Their efforts were unsuccessful each time due to strong opposition from **William III's** forces and most of **the English people**.

352. **William and Mary were crowned the monarchs of England and Ireland** on January 22nd, 1689. This is called **the Convention** Parliament, where those in Parliament were asked to **publicly vote yes or no for the new king and queen**.

353. On April 11th, 1689, **the Convention Parliament** proclaimed **William and Mary the king and queen of Scotland as well.**

354. Even though **Mary was queen alongside her husband**, she had less political influence than him because **women weren't seen as equals to men** during this period.

355. **The Glorious Revolution** also helped to end **the absolute monarchy in England** since **William III and Mary II shared power with Parliament**. This is one reason why **modern Britain has a constitutional monarchy** instead of an absolute one.

356. **This event marked the end of Catholicism** as the official religion in England and Scotland. It ended with an agreement called **the Bill of Rights of 1689**, which established more **freedom for citizens.**

357. **In 1689, William and Mary issued a joint declaration known as the Declaration of Rights,** which stated that all citizens should have certain rights like freedom of speech or trial by jury. These are still fundamental liberties for people living in Britain today.

358. **Parliament passed several laws that limited royal power**, such as forbidding the monarch from suspending laws or raising an army without consent from Parliament. **The monarch also could not set taxes without Parliament's approval.** These limits on government power still exist today.

359. **The Glorious Revolution worried rulers around Europe**. They feared similar revolutions might happen in their countries.

360. **At first, many people were scared that taking away royal power would lead to anarchy,** but surprisingly, it didn't cause any major problems. Instead, it made England more stable than ever before.

361. **After the Glorious Revolution, William III increased English naval power by building new ships** and creating a stronger navy, **which helped England in its wars against France and Spain.**

362. **William allied England with Holland** in an effort to limit the rise of French power.

363. **The king of France from 1643 to 1715 was Louis XIV**. He was perhaps the greatest absolute monarch of all. He was worried that the reforms in England would become popular in his country and **worked hard to destabilize England**. He also created a system of censorship that was aimed at preventing **"dangerous ideas"** (to him) from spreading to his country.

364. **Parliament abolished some taxes** on trading goods and granted more freedoms to merchants, causing economic growth throughout England.

365. **After the Glorious Revolution, William III made some changes to how taxes were collected,** which meant that more money could be raised for the government. These reforms helped make sure there was enough money available for the general welfare if it was needed.

366. **Many historians argue that the Glorious Revolution was one of the most important moments in history** because it **established many basic human rights** like religious tolerance and liberty under the law. These ideas spread throughout the world and are still important today.

367. **The Glorious Revolution period saw England become a worldwide empire**, competing with France for dominance in Europe and the New World.

368. **The freedoms that developed in Britain** during this time were largely responsible for a new political and social movement called **the Enlightenment**, which **inspired the American revolutionaries** and many others.

369. **Before William became king of England, he was known as William of Orange.** Orange refers to a territory his family had controlled for a long time.

370. **Because of his popularity in Holland, the color orange became the national color of that country.**

Age of Enlightenment

(1715–1790)

The Age of Enlightenment was a period of intellectual growth and change in Europe that lasted through most of **the 18th century**. In this section, you'll read about thirty noteworthy facts revealing the development of **new ideas and the invention of new technologies.** We will also explore how people began to think of themselves as **individuals with rights and freedoms.**

371. **The Age of Enlightenment** was a period in history when people started to think more about **science, philosophy, and freedom**.

372. **The Age of Enlightenment** began around 1715 and ended around 1790 when the **French Revolution began.**

373. During this time, some very famous thinkers **like Voltaire and Jean-Jacques Rosseau** wrote books that changed how people thought about **government**, **society**, and **religion**.

374. During this period, **British and French writers and philosophers** greatly affected each other's countries and societies.

375. In **France**, a group of men known as the **Philosophes**, which included **Jean-Jacques Rousseau,** wrote popular books on **politics** and **philosophy** during this period.

376. The ideas of **French and British Enlightenment** thinkers had a profound effect on the **American Founding Fathers** and played a crucial role in starting **the American Revolution.**

377. Many important inventions were made during **the Age of Enlightenment**, such as steam engine technology by **James Watt,** a Scottish inventor. **The steam engine revolutionized transportation in Europe.**

378. **Isaac Newton**, an **English mathematician** who developed **calculus**, was the head of **the Royal Society** from 1703 until his death in 1727. **The Royal Society** still exists today; it is the oldest scientific academic institution in the world!

379. **The Constitution of the United States** was largely based on ideas discussed during **the Age of Enlightenment**, including the new belief that natural rights were held at birth regardless of an individual's class or status in life.

380. **People began questioning traditional ideas about religion during the Age of Enlightenment,** which led to **new religious movements, such as Deism**. Deism is the idea that there is a higher power that created the universe, but this power does not interfere in human affairs and is not affected by a belief in **organized religion.**

381. **The idea of human rights** was **popularized by John Locke**, who wrote ***Two Treatises of Government* in 1690,** which argued for a government based on protecting **individual rights** instead of on power or divine right, the belief that **God puts kings on the throne** and allows them to govern as they see fit.

382. **People also began to think differently about education** during this period. They started believing that **education should be accessible to everyone**, not just the wealthy.

383. **Newspapers gained popularity** due to increased literacy rates, **allowing people to learn more** about what was happening in their countries.

384. **David Hume** was an important **Scottish Enlightenment** writer who **believed that all human knowledge came from experience**, not religious beliefs or God.

385. **Slavery existed in the British colonies until 1833**. Slavery was challenged by a group of people called **abolitionists**, who used arguments from **Enlightenment** philosophers to make a **strong case against slavery.**

386. **Women in England and France** began to slowly gain more rights. This was due to influential women and their works, such as **Mary Wollstonecraft's** 1792 work ***A Vindication of the Rights of Woman.***

387. **Musical styles changed**. Two of the most famous composers of all time, **Mozart and Beethoven, were from this period.**

388. **The Enlightenment** and **the French revolutionary** period that immediately followed it are considered by most historians to **mark the beginning of the modern era.**

389. **This era also saw advances in medicine**. For instance, **English doctor Edward Jenner** invented a **vaccine** for smallpox.

390. **English chemist Joseph Priestley** discovered **oxygen**, which changed how we thought about air!

391. **A new era of European exploration began**. Explorers like **James Cook** mapped out **new lands** and cultures previously unknown to Europeans.

392. **Many Enlightenment philosophers wrote books advocating for democracy**, arguing it would be a better form of government than a monarchy or a government ruled only by the upper classes.

393. **New ideas about economics emerged** from thinkers like **Adam Smith**, a Scottish economist who wrote ***The Wealth of Nations***, which examined **free-market capitalism.**

394. **In France and England**, people in the upper or the rising upper middle class could subscribe to get book series before they were printed. The most famous example is the immensely popular ***Encyclopédie* by Frenchman Denis Diderot**, though many English authors and journals began offering subscriptions.

395. **Coffee houses were popular places** for discussing new ideas about politics, society, and the events of the day.

396. **Coffee houses became so popular that laws were passed to limit how long people could stay in them!**

397. **The first public parks and zoos opened up during this time,** allowing more people access to nature than ever before.

398. **Italian philosopher Cesare Beccaria** wrote about **reforming the criminal justice system in Europe.** Torture was still used in England at this time, and its jails were horrible dungeon-like places.

399. **This era saw an increase in urbanization.** Factories, canals, and other infrastructure projects caused cities to spread out and more people to move to them.

400. Lastly, many European governments, mostly in **western and northern Europe, started giving their citizens greater freedoms**, such as freedom of speech or freedom of the press, which had previously been restricted.

The American Revolution
(1765–1783)

In this section, you'll discover thirty important facts about **the American Revolution from the British point of view.** Learn how the British felt about **the rebellious colonists** and the rights that **King George III** and his government believed they had in the **American colonies**. You'll also learn about the might of the **British armed forces** and why overconfidence was one of the reasons **the British were defeated in the war.**

401. **The British initially viewed the conflict with the American colonies as a minor disturbance rather than a full-scale rebellion**.

402. **The British government believed it had the right to tax the American colonies** to help pay for the cost of defending them during **the French and Indian War** (1754–1763).

403. **King George III** and many British officials saw **the American Revolution** as a betrayal by the colonists, who were considered British subjects.

404. **The British military**, with its highly trained and experienced troops, initially had the upper hand in the early battles of **the American Revolution**.

405. British soldiers, called **Redcoats** (or "Lobsterbacks" by rebels in New England), were often better equipped and more disciplined than **their American counterparts**.

406. **The British strategy focused on capturing major cities** and defeating the Continental Army to force the Americans into submission.

407. **Many British officers and soldiers viewed the American rebels as undisciplined and lacking proper military training**. However, many Americans had to hunt to stay alive and generally were much better shots than British recruits.

408. **Most Americans lived in the countryside** at this time and were familiar with living in the wild, while many British soldiers were not.

409. **The British hired German mercenaries**, known as **Hessians**, to bolster their forces during the war.

410. Most of the troops defeated by **George Washington** and his men at the famous **Battle of Trenton** (1776) **were Hessians, not British**.

411. **The British military** faced significant challenges in transporting troops and supplies **across the Atlantic Ocean**. By the time the men, ships, and supplies were gathered in England and transported across the sea, the situation they faced was different from the message they had received from **British officers asking for help in America**.

412. **The British government struggled to effectively communicate and coordinate with their commanders in America** due to the long distance and slow communication methods.

413. **The British navy, the most powerful in the world at the time,** maintained control of important coastal areas and waterways for most of the war.

414. **General William Howe**, the first British commander-in-chief, believed in a more conciliatory approach toward the colonists and was criticized for not being aggressive enough. **He resigned in 1778, saying the reason was lack of support at home**.

415. **The British underestimated the resolve and determination of the American rebels**, who were fighting for their independence.

416. **The British army faced logistical difficulties in supplying their troops**, especially during the harsh winter months.

417. **British generals often had to contend with conflicting orders from the British government** and disagreements among their own officers.

418. **The British hoped to gain support from Loyalists** (colonists who remained loyal to Britain), but this support was not as widespread as they had anticipated.

419. **The American Revolution exposed divisions** within the British government, with some officials advocating for a more conciliatory approach while others pushed for a harsher military response.

420. **The British faced challenges in recruiting enough troops to fight the war**, leading them to rely on hired mercenaries and colonial Loyalists.

421. **The British government struggled to finance the costly war**, leading to increased taxes and borrowing.

422. **The British army employed scorched-earth tactics** and confiscated property to weaken the rebels' support base. Scorched-earth tactics means burning crops, houses, farms, and businesses to weaken the enemy.

423. **Many American Loyalists fled to Canada during the war and after**. Some historians called **the American Revolution a civil war** because there was much fighting between rebels and Loyalists during the conflict.

424. **The American rebels' use of guerrilla warfare tactics**, including hit-and-run attacks, disrupted British operations and wore down their morale.

425. **The British attempted to implement a blockade of American ports** to restrict trade and weaken the colonial economy.

426. **The Battle of Saratoga in 1777** was a major turning point in the war, as the British suffered a significant defeat.

427. **France, Britain's enemy in Europe, saw that the Americans might win** the war and began sending massive amounts of aid.

428. **The British public grew increasingly weary of the costly and prolonged war**, which ultimately influenced the government's decision to seek a negotiated peace with the United States.

429. **The Treaty of Paris of 1783 ended the American Revolution** in favor of the colonists.

430. **Britain recognized America's independence, and in time**, relations between the two would be repaired. Today, they have a strong and healthy relationship.

The Napoleonic Wars

From 1789 to 1815, **Britain became involved in a great struggle against France**. In 1789, the French people, who had been kept down for centuries by the absolute rule of the French kings and the aristocracy, revolted. **The French Revolution sent shockwaves through Europe, especially England,** which was only miles away from France across the English Channel. After years of chaos and violence in France, **General Napoleon Bonaparte took power and conquered most of Europe.** Though Napoleon had many foes, **his arch-enemy was England.**
Let's take a look at twenty exciting facts about **the Napoleonic Wars.**

431. **The French Revolution** began in the summer of **1789**. **The people of France decided to fight for the rights they had been denied for centuries**, such as the freedom of speech, freedom of the press, and freedom of religion.

432. Though **England** had gone through many similar changes over the years, the aristocracy and the **king still held most of the power.** They were threatened by the ideas of **the French Revolution.**

433. **The French revolutionaries** spread the **ideas of the revolution** to other countries, including England.

434. From 1792 to 1797, **England was part of the First Coalition**, which included other European countries seeking to defeat revolutionary France.

435. From 1798 to 1802, **England was part of another alliance called the Second Coalition,** which attempted to defeat a more successful France and its newest military hero, **General Napoleon Bonaparte.**

436. **Bonaparte rose to fame in France because of his defeat of the British** at the French Mediterranean port of Toulon in 1793 during the War of the First Coalition.

437. Between 1793 and 1804, **Napoleon kept gaining power and support**. By 1800, he was *the* power in France. In 1804, **he was proclaimed emperor of the French.**

438. **Because Britain would not agree to Napoleon's terms for peace, he began what's known as the Continental System.** France and its conquered countries could not trade with Great Britain.

439. **The Continental System eventually backfired on Napoleon** because England traded with many other parts of the world.

440. **The Royal Navy was powerful enough** to ensure that France could not trade with others.

441. **One of England's greatest victories came during the Battle of Trafalgar. English Admiral Nelson,** who was killed in the battle, led the British home fleet against the French Navy. The French were soundly defeated.

442. **Napoleon vowed to conquer England**. He gathered an invasion force of men, ships, landing craft, and even hot air balloons on the French side of the English Channel.

443. However, other events and the money it cost to gather and supply the invasion force while waiting for the right time **made Napoleon give up on the idea of invading England.**

444. **The British had far fewer men in their army than the French, so they were limited in what they could do against Napoleon in Europe**. The British allied themselves with other nations and chose their battles carefully.

445. **In 1808, Napoleon invaded Spain**, which resulted in a long and violent guerrilla war. **England was allied with Portugal**, Spain's neighbor, and landed troops there to fight the French in Spain. **Spain threw Napoleon out in 1814 with England's help**.

446. **In 1812, Napoleon invaded Russia** but was **ultimately defeated by Russia** and the other countries of central Europe that had been previously conquered by Napoleon. In June 1815, **Napoleon's armies were defeated, and he gave up the throne.**

447. **He was exiled to the small island of Elba** in the Mediterranean under British guard.

448. **In February 1815, Napoleon escaped from Elba**, landed in France, and gathered another army. He took over France once again **and launched a war against the Third Coalition.**

449. **At Waterloo in Belgium, Napoleon was defeated for the final time.**

450. **British troops played a central role in Napoleon's final defeat at Waterloo.**

Industrial Revolution

(1760–1850)

The Industrial Revolution was a time **of great change and technological advancement for Britain.** Here are forty interesting facts about that time, though there is much more to learn about this incredible time. **We will explore the invention of new transportation and communication methods,** how the factory system developed, and the positive effects of the railroad. The impacts of **the Industrial Revolution** are still felt worldwide, so let's dig in to find out why!

451. **The Industrial Revolution** was a period of time between **1760 and 1850**, during which **new machines and technologies were developed** to help make production faster and more efficient.

452. **The Industrial Revolution brought about a huge change in how people lived,** worked, ate, traveled, dressed, thought, and communicated with each other.

453. **It also changed where people lived**. Many moved from rural areas into cities to look for factory jobs or better opportunities. **Cities became crowded**. People lived close together in small homes without modern amenities like running water or electricity.

454. **The Enclosure Movement caused a shift in land ownership from small farmers to large landowners**, allowing for increased production of goods on farms using new technologies. Many small farmers were forced to move to cities to make a living.

455. **Inventions like the reaper** allowed farmers to harvest crops much faster than before. The increased crop yields meant lower prices for consumers across Europe.

456. **Improved agricultural techniques** helped increase yields from farmers' fields during this period, leading to greater food security across Europe.

457. **Inventors such as Joseph Priestley, Humphry Davy, Michael Faraday, and Charles Babbage developed new technologies** that spurred industrial growth during this period.

458. During this period, inventions like **the steam engine helped power factories**. Factories made things like cloth and steel on an industrial scale for the first time in history.

459. **New technologies allowed factories**, particularly those located near rivers or canals, **to increase the production of goods.**

460. **In 1764, James Watt, a Scottish inventor, improved the steam engine.** It could produce more power than earlier models, which allowed for more efficient production of goods like textiles and iron products.

461. **Inventors like James Watt developed machines that could harness energy sources in new ways.** Unfortunately, **steam engines used a lot of coal**. By the end of the 19th century, pollution was taking a toll on the health of people, animals, trees, and water. It also **created an almost permanent grey sky over many British cities.**

462. One type of **power unit is called a watt,** as in a 60-watt lightbulb. Watt discovered many things we take for granted today.

463. **Coal mining was transformed due to inventions like hydraulic props,** which supported tunnels underground, and the steam engine, which allowed for deeper, more efficient mines.

464. **Inventions like the cotton gin increased the production of textiles** by allowing larger quantities to be produced at once in factories rather than handcrafted by workers at home. **This had a big impact on employment rates and prices of goods.**

465. **The spinning jenny was invented in 1764 by James Hargreaves**, an English weaver. The spinning jenny could simultaneously spin eight threads instead of just one, making it much faster to produce cloth.

466. **The invention of the power loom in 1785 helped reduce the cost and time it took to produce cloth**, which led to cheaper clothing in stores all over Britain and beyond. **Power looms** were automated machines that could weave faster than humans!

467. **The invention of the Jacquard loom in 1801 made it possible to produce fabrics** with intricate patterns by using punch cards. This was a major advancement over previous **handweaving** methods.

468. **The invention of interchangeable parts made mass production possible as early as 1798.** These components could be assembled into a product without being custom-made each time they were used.

469. **The invention of machine tools like lathes** made precision engineering possible, leading to improved accuracy when producing parts or products.

470. **The new methods of production allowed for the greater production of tools** and consumer goods, as well as weapons for the army and navy.

471. **Improvements in manufacturing processes like mass production allowed for lower prices on items,** such as furniture or clothing, giving consumers access to goods that were previously too expensive.

472. **Early factories were often organized by gender**, with **women doing certain tasks like spinning cotton** while **men operated heavy machinery.**

473. **Many changes took place in the workplace during this time**, with workers beginning to push for better working conditions and shorter hours. However, owners pushed back on many of the workers' ideas.

474. **The Factory Acts of 1802 and 1833** set limits on **how many hours children under nine years old could work in factories.** Before then, there were no restrictions!

475. **Eventually, owners built things like guard rails** around machinery to keep workers safe while they worked. **Miners would gradually start to use metal helmets to protect themselves** from falling rocks and other dangers.

476. **Many people were injured in the new factories**, but there was no unemployment or medical insurance. Many people were reduced to begging and crime to survive.

477. **In England, the murder rate increased because of overcrowded** conditions and because **many crimes were punishable by death**. Since that was the case, many criminals killed witnesses to their crimes.

478. **The Industrial Revolution saw gradual improvements in sanitation**, which helped reduce disease rates. Things like **public water systems**, sewers, and better waste disposal methods were developed during this period.

479. **Gas lighting was invented in 1792**. Over the years, it became more widespread, allowing people to work or travel after dark without having to rely on candles or oil lamps.

480. **The development of more accurate clocks** enabled people to keep track of their working hours, which was important when calculating wages since many jobs were paid by the hour.

481. **Improved banking systems**, such as new investment schemes, encouraged entrepreneurs to pursue many **new business opportunities** during this period.

482. **In 1807, Robert Fulton, an American engineer, invented the first commercially successful steamboat**, allowing large numbers of goods to be shipped up and down rivers quickly.

483. **The development of canals allowed for the more efficient transportation of raw materials** from mines or ports directly into cities where factories could use them. These waterways also provided jobs for many people who worked on building them or navigated boats through them.

484. **The first entirely steam-powered trans-Atlantic voyage was made by the Canadian vessel, the SS *Royal William*, in 1833.**

485. Ships that depended on sails would often stop or slow down when there was little to no wind. **The steamship** eliminated this problem and **made sea travel faster and more reliable.**

486. **The first successful steam locomotive was built by George Stephenson, an English engineer, in 1814. The locomotive revolutionized the transportation** of goods and people across greater distances more quickly.

487. **The construction of railways across Europe enabled goods and people to travel long distances quickly and cheaply**. Railways helped spread ideas from one place to another, leading to greater innovations in other fields, such as **medicine, engineering, and architecture.**

488. **The invention of the telegraph** allowed information to travel rapidly across long distances. **The telegraph was used commercially** as early as 1845.

489. **Improved communication networks, including postal systems and the telegraph**, enabled people from different parts of a country or even from different countries to communicate with each other in ways never seen before.

490. **The Industrial Revolution**, which did not happen outside Europe and North America until much later, marked the beginning of a period of **Western economic and military supremacy throughout the world.**

Slavery and Its Abolition
(1807–1838)

The abolition of the slave trade greatly impacted the lives of the British and those who were enslaved. We'll look at **forty interesting facts about slavery in Britain and its colonies,** including the people who campaigned for abolition and the legacy of the slave trade today.

491. **The slave trade saw English ships travel to West Africa** with goods like guns and clothes, which they used to trade for Africans. **These Africans became enslaved.**

492. **Africans were taken on board ships and then sold in Europe, the Americas, or India. Slaves cost around £20 to £30** per person at this time, which is equivalent to hundreds or even thousands of dollars today.

493. **In 2007, a group of scientists from Liverpool University identified human remains found on board ships that were used for transporting enslaved** Africans across the Atlantic Ocean. This research helped uncover evidence about what life must have been like for those taken away from their homes so long ago.

494. **In 1772, a court in England ruled that slavery was not legal**, but this decision did not stop the slave trade.

495. **In 1807, the British government made a law that said it was illegal to buy or sell people as slaves in Britain and its colonies**. The new law was called the Abolition of the Slave Trade Act. It ended the slave trade but did not end slavery itself.

496. **Before 1807, around one million enslaved Africans lived in Britain's colonies worldwide. Olaudah Equiano** had been enslaved and wrote about his experiences. He helped persuade many people to support **abolition**.

497. **Ignatius Sancho was an enslaved man in England**. He escaped and found refuge with a powerful noble who educated him. **Sancho eventually became a shopkeeper, an abolitionist, and a well-known writer and composer**. He died before the abolition of the slave trade, but his life and writing had a profound effect on attitudes in England.

498. **Many brave campaigners worked** hard to make the abolition of the slave trade happen, including **Thomas Clarkson** and **Granville Sharp. They established the Society for the Abolition of the Slave Trade.**

499. **Many campaigns against the slave trade were done by churches,** such as **Quakers**, **Methodists**, and **Baptists**, whose members actively worked together on pamphlets, petitions, and protests.

500. **Women played an important role in the anti-slavery movement** too, such as **Mary Prince, Elizabeth Heyrick, and Anne Knight**. These women wrote pamphlets or gave speeches encouraging people to stop buying things made with slave labor.

501. **Some campaigners used boycotts to stop businesses from using goods produced with slave labor**. They stopped buying sugar, tobacco, or other items made with slave labor in a process known as **"moral suasion."**

502. **During their campaign against slavery, abolitionists adopted vivid imagery, such as coffins and nooses**, in their publications and demonstrations to help draw attention to the cruelty that slaves endured from the moment they were captured.

503. **William Wilberforce, a prominent abolitionist** MP (member of Parliament), and others campaigned for ten years. They thought the act was the first step toward the abolition of slavery.

504. Even though **the Abolition of the Slave Trade Act** passed, there were still thousands of slaves living in British colonies after 1807.

505. **Between 1796 and 1806, before the end of the British slave trade, it's estimated that about 400,000 slaves were taken captive and sent to work in the West Indies.**

506. One British sailor on a ship assigned to catch slave traders wrote, **"They were in the most dreadful condition that human beings could be in ... I should never have believed that anything could have been so horrible ... Some of them mere walking skeletons."**

507. **The Slave Trade Act also stated that any ships carrying enslaved Africans after this date would be confiscated by the British government**. Their crews would be arrested.

508. **The British Royal Navy formed the West Africa Squadron to intercept slave ships coming from regions where slave ships often departed**. They also formed other squadrons that patrolled other parts of the Atlantic.

509. **The Royal Navy stopped over 1,600 ships carrying an estimated 150,000 enslaved Africans.**

510. **Many of the people freed from slave ships had nowhere to go**. Many areas of Africa did not have officially recognized borders at the time, and most people didn't know where they were from other than in a very general way. **Many people were left in settlements of freed slaves in the West Indies** or formed communities themselves.

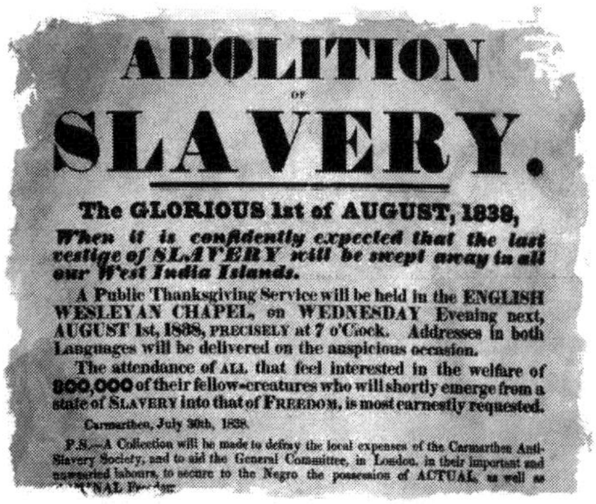

511. **After Britain abolished its slave trade, some African territories started forming their own anti-slavery societies**, campaigning against further enslavement by European countries.

512. **It wasn't until 1833 that another law, the Slavery Abolition Act, finally made it illegal for any person or business to own slaves within Britain's colonies**. This act set all enslaved people free in the British Empire, with the exception of a few of its colonies.

513. **The number of slaves freed in the United Kingdom and its territories was anywhere from 800,000 to a million people.**

514. **It took a very long time for all enslaved Africans living within Britain's colonies to be freed.** Even after 1833, many slaves were simply called "apprentices" and given a small wage to get around the law.

515. **Some people didn't believe slavery was wrong and kept slaves even though it was illegal.** These people were called "illegal traders" and could be jailed if they were caught.

516. **This act also provided compensation for those who lost money when they had to free their slaves.**

517. **Britain paid over twenty million pounds to former slave owners**, which was about 40 percent of the British budget.

518. **Some former plantation owners turned their land into sugar refining factories using new technologies**, and other former slave traders tried new ways of making money, such as investing in cotton mills or setting up trading companies that dealt with goods from Africa, like palm oil.

519. **Some sugar plantations replaced enslaved Africans with indentured laborers from India or China.** These workers signed contracts lasting five to seven years. Almost all of them were paid less than half of what freemen earned.

520. **Indentured servants came from all over the British Empire, including Ireland.**

521. **In the 18th and 19th centuries, many British prisoners were sent to the sugarcane fields in the Caribbean**, where many perished from the climate, disease, and mistreatment.

522. **Though the United Kingdom was one of the first countries to ban slavery, Denmark and Norway banned the slave trade in 1803.**

523. **Even after 1833, many countries worldwide still allowed slavery, such as France, which abolished slavery in 1848. The United States didn't abolish it until 1865.**

524. **Many Africans welcomed Britain's decision to abolish slavery**. They saw it as an opportunity for freedom and self-determination.

525. **Today, monuments and museums throughout Britain and other countries worldwide are dedicated to remembering those affected by the slave trade** and celebrating freedom from slavery, such as **the International Slavery Museum in Liverpool**, England, a port city and the center of the slave trade before abolition.

526. **In 1833, there was a huge celebratory march through London's streets** when news spread that slavery had been abolished in Britain and its colonies. Thousands joined together for this event, now known as the Abolition Parade.

527. **In 2007, Britain celebrated two hundred years since abolition** with various events held throughout the country, including special exhibitions in museums, plays, and concerts for people to learn more about this important moment in history.

528. **Though slavery was abolished in the UK in 1833, African Britons faced considerable discrimination and prejudice**, which is still an issue in much of the UK.

529. **There were still discriminatory laws on the books in Britain** until the middle of the 20th century. Even after laws were passed, many black English people were discriminated against in housing and the job market.

530. **In more recent times, British prime ministers and the government have issued apologies for the era of slavery**.

Reform Acts

(1832–1867)

The Reform Acts were a series of laws passed in Britain with the aim of bringing about a more equal and representative government for its people. Let's look at thirty facts about **how the Reform Acts affected the country**, including how voting and parliamentary representation changed.

531. **People had been protesting for reform since the 1640s**, but it wasn't until the 1830s that the government started listening.

532. **This period from 1832 to 1867 is sometimes called the Age of Reform** because so many laws were passed during this time to improve how government worked and how people voted.

533. **The Reform Act of 1832 was the first law passed in Britain that allowed small property holders to vote for representatives in Parliament.**

534. **Before the Reform Act, only 2 percent of British citizens could vote**. They were mostly wealthy landowners.

535. Before this reform bill, **Britain's political system had been largely based on a patronage system,** where MPs were elected by rich landowners who held most of the power.

536. **Most of the power had rested with the aristocracy**, but as the changes of the Industrial Revolution progressed, a new, more numerous and wealthy middle class began to gain power and influence.

537. **The Reform Act of 1832 created a new set of qualified voters known as "forty-shilling freeholders,"** who could vote if they paid more than forty shillings in rent or taxes each year.

538. **The Reform Act extended voting rights from just a few hundred thousand people to over 600,000 people**. These people could now elect members of Parliament (MPs).

539. **The Reform Act also changed how seats were allocated in Parliament** by making regions or constituencies more equal based on population size and wealth.

540. **It also gave some representation to cities and industrial areas** that had previously been underrepresented or not represented at all.

541. **The act allowed for some of the larger cities, such as Birmingham and Manchester, to gain representation in Parliament**, ending rules that had kept them from being represented.

542. **As part of this act, small borough constituencies with fewer than one thousand voters lost their seats**. Larger borough constituencies gained or absorbed them. As a result, more MPs began representing urban areas instead of rural ones.

543. **The Reform Act was designed to stop "rotten boroughs"** from having undue influence over Parliament. Rotten boroughs were constituencies with very few voters that still had representation in Parliament.

544. **By reducing the number of "rotten boroughs,"** the country saw more fairness and made voting easier for many citizens.

545. **In addition, it defined how constituencies would be redrawn every ten years in case of population shifts.**

546. **This law ensured that each constituency had enough people registered to vote** so their voices would be heard and represented fairly, though it was a slow process.

547. **Limits began to be put on the upper house of Parliament, the House of Lords**, which was made up of men from old aristocratic, titled families.

548. **The Reform Act also gave the government some responsibility** for ensuring that elections were fair and free from corruption or bribery.

549. **Many new industries, or rather their owners, were better represented in Parliament.** Previously, they had no voice whatsoever in Parliament.

550. **While this act increased voting rights considerably, certain groups were still excluded, including women** and those who did not own property or pay sufficient taxes.

551. It's important to remember that **the movement toward equality, complete representation, and openness in government was a slow process**. Change didn't happen overnight. It wasn't **until after World War One** that men and women from social groups other than the aristocracy had meaningful representation and power.

552. **This legislation is often called the *Great* Reform** Act because it was an incredibly important piece of legislation that **changed British politics forever.**

553. **The laws in the Reform Act of 1832** were perhaps the most radical legal and political changes since the Magna Carta (1215) and the Glorious Revolution of 1689.

554. One of the things that happened during this time was that **many districts were recreated to include roughly the same amount of people**, with only one member representing each district. This was the main focus of the Third Reform Act of 1884.

555. In addition, **due to complicated registration processes, some eligible voters were discouraged and did not take part**, which is what some people had hoped would happen.

556. **When the Third Reform Act was passed, about 40 percent of men had the right to vote.** Women could not vote at this time. Many districts and regions had their own rules about who could vote, mainly based on old, out-of-date laws and traditions.

557. **The Representation of the People Acts that were passed between 1918 and 1928 allowed even more people to vote, including women.**

558. **After the Reform Act of 1832 passed, Britain's two-party system began forming,** which is essentially how the British political landscape looks today.

559. **Separate acts were passed in Ireland and Scotland called the Irish and Scottish Reform Acts.** They made similar changes in those areas, though not completely, especially in Ireland, where many people were hostile to British rule. **In many places, the Irish could not vote. Others refused to vote, as they saw the British as an occupying force.**

560. **Although there were some limitations on who could actually vote due to property requirements**, overall, **the Reform Act led Britain toward a more democratic system** where citizens had a say in their government.

SECTION 2: Uncovering Britain Beginning with the Victorian Era

Victorian Era

(1837–1901)

We have arrived **at the Victorian era, a period of great social, political, and technological change. Queen Victoria was on the throne. The Industrial Revolution** changed the way people worked and lived. And **Great Britain was one of the world's most powerful countries**. So much happened during these **sixty-four years**. Let's look at thirty fascinating facts about **this famous era** in history.

561. **The Victorian era was named after Queen Victoria**. She had a powerful influence on British society during this time.

562. Until **Queen Elizabeth II's** death in 2022, **Queen Victoria** had been the longest reigning monarch in British history, ruling for **sixty-three years and seven months**, from 1837 to 1901.

563. **During the Victorian era, Britain became one of the most powerful countries in the world. Its vast empire included India, Canada, and parts of Africa and Asia**.

564. One of the many **titles Queen Victoria** held was **Empress of India**. The United Kingdom controlled much of the Indian subcontinent.

565. **Great Britain and France almost went to war with each other in 1898 over a territorial dispute in East Africa**, where they both claimed colonies.

566. The Victorian era did see war, though. **The Crimean War** (1853–1856) was a conflict between **Russia and an alliance of Britain, France, the Ottoman Empire** (Turkey), and **Sardinia**.

567. **Queen Victoria's husband, Prince Albert, co-organized the Great Exhibition of 1851 with Henry Cole, the inventor of the Christmas card**. The exhibition showcased products from around the world, including new inventions like **steam engines, sewing machines,** and much more.

568. **The telephone, typewriter, and phonograph were all developed during this era.**

569. **Newspapers, phonographs, photos, and much else all helped to bring more common threads to the people of Britain,** which became more united at this time.

570. **Photography was developed in the second part of the 19th century**. This allowed people to record personal and public events like weddings and wars.

571. **Queen Victoria popularized wearing white wedding dresses, which became the standard for brides around the world.**

572. **Scottish-born American Alexander Graham Bell invented the telephone**, allowing people to quickly communicate over large distances and get emergency help. The telephone was expensive for many years. Only wealthier people owned one.

573. **The Penny Black stamp went into circulation in 1840**, allowing people to send letters across long distances quickly for a penny.

574. **Railways linked most parts of Britain together**, which made traveling easier than ever. **Trains became the preferred mode of transport** for people traveling between cities.

575. **Expanding railways** and the growth of cities meant that large groups of people were meeting and interacting with people from distant parts of the country for the first time.

576. **The underground rail system opened in London in 1863**, revolutionizing transportation around cities and making it more efficient than ever before.

577. **Electric lighting was introduced**, which made it easier to work at night without having to use gas lamps or candles.

578. **Street lighting became common throughout Europe**, allowing people to move around safely at night with less fear of being mugged or attacked by criminals.

579. **Despite street lights and the development of a professional police force**, many English cities suffered from increased crime rates during this period.

580. **The changes brought by the Industrial Revolution made some men and families incredibly wealthy**. Many of these people were not aristocrats. They were members of the rising middle class, which would play a greater role in Britain from this point on.

581. **Agricultural production increased due to mechanization**, resulting in much higher yields.

582. **Laws were passed that limited child labor**, with factories having specific laws about how old a child had to be before they could work. **More children gradually began attending grade school for free.**

583. **The sewing machine was invented**, making it easier for women at home or working in factories to make clothing.

584. **Women's rights advanced significantly during the Victorian era**. They gained more access to education opportunities and some legal rights like **owning property or inheriting land without permission from a male relative.**

585. **Life expectancy increased significantly** due to better sanitation standards and advances in medicine, though the inner cities of England, especially in bigger cities like London, were dangerous, unhealthy, and crowded places for a long time.

586. **Advances in science, such as pasteurization, were made during this time**, which led to improved sanitation standards around Europe and America.

587. **Charles Darwin published his famous book *On the Origin of Species* in 1859**, which proposed evolution by natural selection.

588. **The Victorian era was called the Golden Age of English Literature**. **Charles Dickens, George Eliot, Thomas Hardy,** and many other famous authors wrote novels during this time.

589. **Three of Victoria's grandchildren were kings in Europe when WWI began**: **George V of England, Wilhelm II of Germany**, and **Nicholas II of Russia**, who were all cousins.

590. **By the time of Victoria's death in 1901, Britain had colonies or territories around the globe. Around 25 percent of the world was controlled by Great Britain**. Many of the world's oceans were dominated by the British Royal Navy. A popular saying was, **"The sun never sets on the British Empire."**

The Great Exhibition

(1851)

The Great Exhibition of 1851 was a fascinating event that showed off the wealth and power of Great Britain. People could see **the Crystal Palace** or the thousands of exciting objects on display. **This event had an incredible impact on people across the world;** let's see how.

591. **The Great Exhibition of 1851 was the world's first international exhibition. It was held in London.**

592. **It took place in a building called the Crystal Palace,** which had over 990,000 square feet of display space!

593. **Over one hundred countries sent items to be displayed at the Great Exhibition**. The exhibition showcased art and items from all around the world!

594. **The exhibition was a reflection of a more interconnected world with Britain** at its center.

595. **A grand opening ceremony marked the start of the Great Exhibition**. **Queen Victoria arrived on horseback accompanied by her husband, Prince Albert**, as well as their seven children. They were all dressed in white.

596. **Over six million people visited it during its six-month run**. That was about one-third of Britain's population at that time.

597. **The Great Exhibition became "the place to be" for members of British society**.

598. Many famous figures attended the exhibition, including **Charles Dickens** and **Michael Faraday**, both of whom gave lectures while they were there.

599. **Special steam engines were set up outside so visitors could travel easily by train directly into Hyde Park**, where the exhibition was located.

600. **To make sure visitors didn't get lost while they explored all the wonders, special maps were made of the Crystal Palace's** interior, complete with street names like Regent Street or Oxford Street after famous London locations.

601. **Interpreters from different countries were hired so visitors could ask questions** about items in their own native tongue.

602. **The Great Exhibition was the first time many people got to experience international cuisine.** A variety of food from around the world was available, including **Indian curries, Chinese noodles**, and **Turkish delights.**

603. **It was also the first time that most people saw exotic items like ostrich feathers, Japanese lacquers, and kangaroo leather products.**

604. **Thirteen thousand items were displayed at the Great Exhibition**, including the famous **Koh-i-Noor diamond**, which weighed **186 carats**. The diamond was just under one pound!

605. **One popular attraction at the exhibition was life-sized dolls that could move their eyes and mouths**. These mechanical marvels were surprisingly lifelike for the time.

606. One of the most famous attractions **at the Great Exhibition was a giant water fountain** that could shoot jets up to forty feet in the air!

607. **To show off Britain's industrial might, different areas of the Great Exhibition showcased items like steam engines and heavy machinery produced by British companies.** These objects were found in an area called the Machinery Hall.

608. **As well as having displays inside on topics like engineering and industry, the Crystal Palace also boasted a huge garden area** outside featuring exotic plants imported for the event.

609. **Every evening during the Great Exhibition, performances would be put on by bands that played traditional music from different countries.**

610. **The Great Exhibition is seen by many historians as a kind of "coming-out party" for Great Britain.** The exhibition made it clear that Britain was the preeminent economic and cultural capital of the world, as well as a great military power.

Crimean War

(1853–1856)

The Crimean War was fought between Britain, Russia, Turkey, France, and Sardinia. Why did they fight? For control of **the Crimean Peninsula, the Caucasus region, and the Baltic Sea.** There are so many interesting facts about this war, including **the daring Charge of the Light Brigade**, the introduction of **new military tactics**, the use of new technologies, and so much more.

611. **The Crimean War was fought between Russia and an alliance of France, Britain, the Ottoman Empire (Turkey), and the Kingdom of Sardinia (in modern Italy).**

612. **One of the reasons Britain and France allied with Turkey was because they were afraid that Russia would dominate the region since** Turkey was not as strong as it once had been.

613. **Although France had mainly entered into this conflict because of its alliance with Britain,** it also wanted control over Syria, which Russia had been trying to gain access to.

614. **The war lasted from October 1853 to February 1856.**

615. The most important battle of the war was **the Siege of Sevastopol** (1854–1855).

616. During a battle near **Sevastopol**, an entire regiment of **elite French Zouaves** ("zwah-vays") charged into Russian lines while singing the French anthem**, "La Marseillaise."** They inspired other troops with their bravery, despite suffering terrible losses themselves.

617. Another famous engagement took place at **Inkerman in 1854**. A small force of **British soldiers** held off nearly ten times their number for several hours before reinforcements arrived, earning them recognition for their courage under fire.

618. **During the Battle of Balaclava in October 1854**, a group of British soldiers held off an entire Russian division for over three hours. They became known as the **"Thin Red Line." Their bravery was honored with six Victoria Crosses**, the highest military decoration in Great Britain.

619. **At Balaclava, Lord Cardigan led his cavalry on what is called the "Charge of the Light Brigade,"** which became the subject of songs and stories, even though it was a British defeat.

620. **When the Crimean War first began, British soldiers wore elaborate uniforms, similar in many ways to what the queen's or king's guards at Buckingham Palace** wear today. They looked great on the parade ground but were incredibly hot, too colorful, and not tough enough to withstand conditions on the battlefield. Many British troops took what they could from dead Russian soldiers or traded with their allies for better uniforms.

621. **The use of the telegraph allowed the British to move their troops rapidly** to where they were needed most.

622. **The British Navy blockaded Russian ports,** preventing ships carrying supplies or reinforcements from entering or leaving, leading to shortages and **weakening Russia's position.**

623. **The Crimean War was the first major conflict where railways were used for military purposes.** Trains transported troops, ammunition, and supplies across vast distances quickly, allowing for more efficient movements of armies around Europe.

624. **In March 1855, the autocratic Russian emperor, Nicholas I, died and was replaced by the more liberal Alexander II**.

625. **In November 1855, Russia agreed to peace negotiations**. But before any treaty could be signed, hostilities broke out again, lasting until **March 1856** when both sides finally reached a compromise.

626. **Before the war, most armies used older weapons, such as muskets, which took a long time to load and fire.** During this conflict, some forces started using new weapons that could shoot much faster.

627. **British inventor Henry Bessemer developed a new kind of artillery shell**, but the cannons couldn't handle it well. After the war, Bessemer developed what's known as the **Bessemer process**, which allowed for the mass production of higher-quality steel.

628. **This conflict saw some advances in military engineering**, like trench-building techniques and the large-scale use of mobile artillery. Both of these innovations would **later become integral parts of WWI battlefield strategies**.

629. **During this conflict, soldiers from all countries wrote letters home describing their experiences.** Many of these correspondences were later published in books and newspapers, giving us valuable insight into what life on the front line was really like.

630. **This war was the first time that photography was used** to document a conflict. **Roger Fenton famously took photographs of the battlefields** and armies during his visits there in 1855 and again in 1856.

631. **The Crimean War was the first major international conflict** to be covered by newspapers, providing an unprecedented level of public awareness about this war's events.

632. **Several important inventions came out of this conflict**, such as improved **ambulance wagons**, which were designed specifically for transporting wounded soldiers from battlefields. **Medical tents** were also set up near the front lines so injured men could receive treatment quickly.

633. **The Crimean War saw some advances in medical science too**. **Anesthetics** were used for surgery for the first time during combat operations by British surgeons working in the field.

634. **Improvements in medical hygiene made during the Crimean War would later influence the Union Army's hospitals during the American Civil War.**

635. **Florence Nightingale** became famous for her work as **a nurse during this war**. She helped improve hospital conditions for wounded soldiers on both sides of the conflict.

636. **Americans were deeply interested in the Crimean War** for many reasons. One of the groups most interested were doctors, some of whom journeyed to Crimea **to study battlefield medicine** and ways it could be improved. **Many of these changes were implemented in the US during the Civil War.**

637. **In total, there were over 600,000 casualties from all sides during this conflict.** Around **250,000 of those died due to disease** or other causes unrelated to the fighting, such as cold weather or poor sanitation practices.

638. **The Treaty of Paris of 1856 ended this war**. **It regulated trade between Russia and other European countries** and established a neutral zone in the Black Sea and its coastline. No one could build ships or fortifications there without permission from the nations who signed the treaty.

639. **The terms of the peace treaty were largely drawn up by Britain and France. Since Turkey was the weakest partner, it benefited the least.**

640. **The official language used in negotiations between Russia and Britain at one point was French,** even though both nations had representatives present who could speak English or Russian fluently!

641. **The Treaty of Paris ended more than just hostilities between Russia and the Allied forces.** It also redrew many borders across Europe, including those separating **Austria and Hungary along the Danube River.**

642. **Though the war was fought in the Crimean Peninsula,** Russia lost land on its western border in the treaty that ended the war.

643. **Although Britain had entered the war mainly due to concerns about Russian expansion into Ottoman territories,** it increased its influence over those same lands after the conflict.

644. **The British and Russians struggled with each other over control of Afghanistan in the 1870s and 1880s.**

645. **Because of British domination, its increased power in Ottoman territories, and its disputes with France in Africa, many foreigners called England "Perfidious Albion." "Albion"** is an old name for England, and **"perfidious"** means **"untrustworthy."**

646. **In the second part of the 19th century, Britain greatly expanded its power and influence**. Some historians view the Crimean War as one of the major reasons to its rise in power.

647. **After the war ended, a number of monuments were erected to commemorate those who had lost their lives**. One of the most famous is **the Valley of Death in Sevastopol,** where over ten thousand soldiers from both sides are buried together as brothers-in-arms.

648. **One of the Russian soldiers involved in the war was a young Leo Tolstoy,** who is arguably **the greatest Russian writer**. The observations he made while serving as an artillery officer during the Siege of Sebastopol became key parts of his most famous work, ***War and Peace*.**

649. **Florence Nightingale was the most famous woman of the war**, but others came to help, including a biracial woman from Jamaica named **Mary Jane Seacole**, who became known as **the "Creole with the tea mug"** for supplying tired and wounded troops with some of the comforts of home. **"Creole"** is an old term for someone of Caucasian and African descent in the Western Hemisphere.

650. **When the war ended, Russia was almost broke and needed cash and gold badly.** This was one reason **the Russians sold Alaska to the United States** in 1854.

Irish Potato Famine

(1845–1850)

The Irish Potato Famine, also called the Great Famine, was a period of **great suffering and loss of life in Ireland.** Many **Irish families migrated to America** because of it. What caused this massive famine? How did it shape Irish culture and the culture of the countries those immigrants landed in? **How could a potato blight spread so quickly and destroy so much more than the plants in the ground?** Why was the British government so slow to respond?

This famine is still remembered today and has been used as a symbol of resilience and determination in the face of adversity. Let's explore forty facts about this terrible event in history and **the relationship between the Irish and the English.**

651. **Contact between England and Ireland went back centuries before the 19th century.** Christianity spread more quickly in Ireland than in England, and many **early evangelists in England were Irish monks.**

652. **Ireland had the same issues as England when it came to the Vikings.** The Vikings took over much of Ireland's coastline but could not spread inland due to fierce resistance.

653. **Over time, a new culture, a mix of Irish and Norse, spread in coastal Ireland called Hiberno-Norse. Hibernia** was the Roman name for Ireland.

654. **The English began their domination of Ireland in 1169 when a revolt against Henry II by his sons and ex-wife, Eleanor of Aquitaine, broke out there**. Henry's family allied themselves with powerful Irish chieftains against Henry but were defeated.

655. From the mid-16th century until 1625, **English and Scottish lords were granted huge areas of Ireland by the English monarchy**, forcing the Irish out.

656. **In 1601, a Spanish force landed in Ireland, hoping to rally their fellow Catholics against English and Scottish Protestant rule**. The English defeated the Spanish and took formal control of Ireland from 1603 until 1921. **In 1921, the southern part of Ireland (the Republic of Ireland) gained independence.**

657. Much of what is Northern Ireland today was settled by Scottish and English Protestants, along with a number of local Irish Protestants. Today, **Northern Ireland is still part of the UK.**

658. **In 1798, the Irish Rebellion occurred. It spread from Dublin into the countryside and then throughout the country**. The rebels wanted an end to English rule, and many attacks on Protestants took place, resulting in a cycle of revenge. **The rebellion was forcibly ended in October 1798, six months after it began.**

659. **During the late 18th century and into the 19th century, the English began a concerted campaign to destroy the Irish language**. The language was a key part of Irish identity and reminded the Irish of their history.

660. **As a result of English and Scottish lords claiming much of Ireland as their own, many Irish were forced off their farms and into factories**. Many went to England and the United States in search of opportunities but faced discrimination.

661. **Large Irish communities exist in many cities in England,** especially in the northwest.

662. **In 1845, the Irish Potato Famine began**. It lasted until 1850 and changed Ireland forever.

663. **The Irish Potato Famine had a major impact on the population of Ireland**. The population decreased by over 20 percent between 1841 and 1851 due to death or emigration.

664. **Over one million people died during this time**, while **another two million left their homes and emigrated to other countries,** such as Canada, Australia, New Zealand, the United States, and England.

665. **The US has more people of Irish descent than Ireland does**. This is largely because of the Potato Famine.

666. **The famine was caused by a fungus known as *Phytophthora infestans***, which attacked potatoes all over Europe. **The fungus impacted Ireland the most due to the country's high dependence on potatoes as its main food source.**

667. It is believed that one of the main factors behind why the blight spread so quickly across Ireland was **that many farmers planted only one type of potato, which made them more susceptible to disease.**

668. **One-third to one-half of all potatoes grown during this period were diseased**. Even if farmers managed to save some crops, they often ended up having rotten potatoes instead.

669. **Poor nutrition levels combined with poor sanitation meant that people not only died of hunger but also suffered from diseases.**

670. **The British government didn't do enough to help those affected** by the famine or provide relief efforts even though they knew what was going on since reports started coming out about it soon after it started.

671. **In 1845, Ireland exported more than three million tons of grain,** yet the British colonial government still failed to provide relief efforts or put an end to grain exports, which further contributed to **the suffering and starvation of the Irish.**

672. **In 1847, an act was passed by the British government to provide relief efforts to those affected by the famine.** However, this relief came too late and had little effect on reducing deaths or stopping emigration out of Ireland.

673. **In 1845, the British Whig government created 700,000 jobs for Irishmen**. They were poorly paid but made enough to keep them and a small family from starvation. Unfortunately, this program was cut when **the conservative Tory Party came back into power, costing the lives of many Irish.**

674. **During the famine, charity organizations, such as Quakers, provided much-needed relief efforts,** including soup kitchens, medical care, and temporary housing for displaced people.

675. **In some areas, potato stocks were buried underground so they could be used later on,** but many of them ended up rotting because there weren't enough people left to eat them.

676. **Much of the best land in Ireland was held by British aristocrats and their Protestant Irish compatriots.** What land was left over was held by the common people, but plots were often so small that the only crop that would grow in sufficient numbers was potatoes.

677. **Due to an increase in poverty levels after the famine, many children were forced into workhouses** where they worked long hours under harsh conditions for little or no pay.

678. **Many people turned toward crime or prostitution to survive,** which led to an increase in crime rates across Ireland.

679. **In order to survive, people turned toward crime or prostitution, while others joined militias such as Ribbonmen and Whiteboys,** who used violence against landlords due to their harsh evictions and waged a small-scale guerrilla war against Irish Protestants. This war would grow throughout the rest of the century until Ireland won its independence in 1921.

680. **Irish painter Daniel Macdonald (1821–1853) recorded the misery of the famine in his many paintings.** In 1847, his paintings were exhibited in London, bringing increased attention to the suffering in Ireland.

681. **The Great Potato Famine not only impacted those who lived through it but has been used as an example in history books ever since to illustrate how important food security is.**

682. **To try to prevent other famines from occurring, governments in Europe began introducing laws that restricted grain exports and imposed heavy taxes on landowners** so that they could not keep food from those who needed it.

683. **After the potato blight had passed, new crop strains were developed that allowed for greater yields.**

684. **The potato blight has been known to reoccur sporadically** ever since its initial outbreak, most recently in the 1970s. Potatoes were affected again, but luckily, no large-scale famines have occurred since then.

685. **Despite the Irish Potato Famine's tragic consequences, there have been some positive effects** from it, such as increased economic opportunities abroad for many Irish immigrants who often couldn't find work or a decent wage at home.

686. **The Irish Potato Famine greatly contributed to a rise in Irish nationalism**, with many people wanting independence from British rule after seeing how little help was provided to them.

687. **The Great Hunger Memorial, located at Battery Park in New York City, is dedicated to all those lost during this tragedy** and serves as a reminder of how important it is to offer aid when disasters occur.

688. **One of the institutions the English installed in Ireland to "discourage" poverty and unemployment was the workhouse**. The workhouse was a place with a bed, enough food to survive, and a little pay for a lot of work.

689. **Many Irish families sold what little they owned and tried to get into the few workhouses in the country**. However, the workhouses filled quickly, and the government refused to build more since they didn't want the Irish to get used to British "welfare."

690. **The Irish Potato Famine has been recorded in many books over the years** and is still remembered today as a major tragedy.

The Boer Wars

(1880–1881 and 1899–1902)

Now we'll explore **the late 19th-century Boer Wars**, which were two conflicts fought between **the British Empire and the two independent Boer republics: the Orange Free State and the South African Republic.** Learn thirty interesting facts about the military tactics used and the aftermath of the conflicts. **Modern South Africa was shaped by these wars.** Let's learn how!

691. **The Boer Wars were fought between the British Empire and the Dutch settlers in South Africa who called themselves the Boers.**

692. **The Boers were descendants of the original Dutch colonists** who settled in South Africa in 1652.

693. **The British began to settle in southern Africa in the early 19th century**. The Dutch and the British fought costly wars against the dominant tribe in the area, **the Zulu**, who fought other tribes for control of much of **eastern and southeastern South Africa**.

694. **In 1879, the British and the Boers were allied against the Zulu**. The British and the Boers were successful, marking the start of a long policy that eventually ended in a racially segregated country for most of the 20th century: **the Republic of South Africa.**

695. **The Boer Wars were part of a larger program of British expansion in Africa** during the second half of the 19th century. **By 1900, most of Africa was controlled by Britain and France. Germany, Belgium, Italy, and Portugal** controlled smaller parts.

696. **The First Boer War was between Great Britain and two independent South African republics:** the **Transvaal Republic** (Zuid-Afrikaansche Republiek or ZAR, meaning South African Republic) and **the Orange Free State** (OFS). The war lasted from 1880 to 1881.

697. **There were many causes for the war, including British immigration**, a belief that **the British were pushing the Boers** out of the territory they considered their own, and unfair taxation on the Boers by the British government.

698. **The Boer Wars saw the use of new tactics, such as trench warfare.** Soldiers would dig deep trenches to protect themselves from incoming fire. **Trench warfare** wasn't as effective as it could be since soldiers often had to rebuild the trenches after each battle.

699. **Many historians argue that the use of trenches greatly increased civilian suffering** since anyone found near these fortifications could be arrested without trial.

700. **The standard British uniform consisted of a red jacket, blue pants with a red stripe, and a white safari or pith helmet**, which made them stand out in the African landscape. **The Boers, most of whom were hunters and very good shots**, were able to easily spot the British.

701. **In 1899, the Second Anglo-Boer War or the South African War began** when three separate Boer governments declared independence from Great Britain: **the Transvaal Republic, the Orange Free State, and Goshen**, the latter of which was a short-lived republic near modern-day Botswana.

702. **Paul Kruger served as president of the Transvaal Republic** during the Second Anglo-Boer War. He refused to surrender even when his own people started running out of resources.

703. **One of the most influential people in the Second Boer War was Cecil Rhodes**, who provided financial support to Britain's military forces. **He even formed his own paramilitary organization known as the Rhodesia Regiment**, which fought alongside regular troops. **The Rhodes Scholarship is named after Cecil Rhodes.**

704. **Another famous man from the Second Boer War was Winston Churchill**. Churchill was a former **soldier in South Africa** who became a journalist. He was captured after an intense battle. **Churchill escaped the prisoner-of-war camp** he was in and traveled hundreds of miles to freedom. When he was finally free, he was greeted with a huge hero's welcome in London.

705. **The man who took Churchill prisoner was P. W. Botha**, who later became **the leader of South Africa's Imperial Army** and an ally of England during WWII. **Botha eventually became South Africa's first independent president.**

706. **Another recognizable figure of the Boer Wars was Mahatma Gandhi**. He worked as an ambulance driver for British forces. **He also spread his philosophy of nonviolence** and civil disobedience through his writings at this time.

707. Many women fought alongside men during the Boer Wars, including **Emily Hobhouse,** who ran supplies between different camps while dodging enemy fire. **She also wrote several books** discussing her experiences there before becoming a famous British suffragette later in life.

708. During these wars, several secret societies sprung up with the goal of gaining independence for **the Transvaal Republic** (ZAR) and **Orange Free State** (OFS). Two examples are **the Afrikanerbond and Het Volk**, whose members included future president **Paul Kruger**. They would later take part in a successful revolt against British rule known as **the Rebellion of 1914**.

709. **During the Second Boer War, many women and children were placed in internment camps by British forces**, which caused a lot of suffering and claimed many lives. **The internment of Boer civilians put pressure on the Boers to make peace with Britain.**

710. **To gain support from other countries, both sides sent diplomats overseas**. Boer diplomats spread tales about their own people's suffering under British rule in an attempt **to win sympathy for their cause**.

711. **African tribes living close by took part in some engagements against British forces during both wars**. They were often hired by local chiefs who wanted revenge on their former oppressors.

712. **After failing to defeat the Boers directly, British forces decided to use a scorched-earth policy**, which involved destroying crops and farms owned by Dutch settlers so they wouldn't have enough supplies.

713. **The British sent messages to as many Boer farms and areas as they could to cause slaves to flee and fight for Britain**, which had outlawed slavery. The Boers still held slaves in the territories under their control.

714. **In 1900, some towns, such as Mafeking, were declared independent from Great Britain** when they refused to accept surrender terms offered by General Frederick Roberts at that time. **The townspeople eventually gave in after 217 days because of the lack of food supplies** caused by the siege.

715. **Many British people were horrified by what happened during the siege of Mafeking and put pressure on their government to end the war.**

716. In 1901, a group of Africans that called themselves **"the Peaceful Revolution" started peaceful protests throughout the Transvaal Republic** (ZAR) and **Orange Free State** (OFS) in hopes of gaining independence from Great Britain. Although they failed to achieve their goal due to the lack of support from other countries, many historians believe **their actions inspired later civil rights movements around the world.**

717. **In 1902, just three years after Queen Victoria's death, Britain signed a treaty with the Transvaal Republic** (ZAR) and **the Orange Free State** (OFS), ending the Second Boer War.

718. **After the war ended in 1902, both sides signed a treaty that granted the Transvaal Republic (ZAR) and the Orange Free State (OFS) independence from Great Britain.** However, they were still part of the Union of South Africa. **The Union of South Africa ended in 1961 when the union became a republic.**

719. **Britain gained control over what is now known as the Union of South Africa**, which included **the modern-day countries of Lesotho, Botswana, Namibia, and Zimbabwe.**

720. **After the war ended in 1902, an estimated fifty thousand Boers died either due to combat or disease**. Twenty-two thousand British soldiers were killed during the conflict.

World War I

(1914–1918)

World War I was a global conflict between the Allied Powers and the Central Powers. More than **sixty-five million soldiers from thirty countries fought in the war**. The war saw **the first major use of tanks, airplanes, submarines, and chemical weapons,** resulting in about **forty million casualties**, with anywhere from **fifteen to twenty million dead.** This chapter will explore forty sobering facts about the conflict, including the **weapons used, the battles fought, and the war's impact on society**.

721. **The Triple Alliance of Germany, Austria-Hungary, and Turkey** faced off **against the Triple Entente of Britain, France, and Russia in World War I**. Later, **Italy** and **the United States joined the Allies** (the Triple Entente).

722. **The reasons for the war are many, but the immediate cause was the assassination of Austrian Archduke Franz Ferdinand by Serbian nationalists in Bosnia**. Once that happened, **Serbia and Austria mobilized their armies**, leading their allies to do the same. War was declared in 1914.

723. **Britain and France were interested in stopping the ever-more powerful Germany from dominating Europe.**

724. **European nations used propaganda to try and win the hearts and minds of their citizens to gain support for the war effort**. They used posters, newspapers, radio broadcasts, and even movies.

725. **Many British women served near the front lines as nurses during the war**. Like it did for many men, the intensity of the first major war of the 20th century stunned and horrified them.

726. **At home, many women worked in factories, making weapons and supplies**. **WWI provided many employment opportunities for women,** who filled roles vacated by men who had gone off to fight overseas. **Women built tanks and aircraft. They drove buses and trains.** They also handled administrative duties within army units, giving them greater freedom than ever before.

727. **On Christmas Day, 1914, British and German soldiers laid down their arms in some areas along the Western Front so they could celebrate together peacefully**. This event became known as **"the Christmas Truce" or "the Silent Night Truce."**

728. **The British, along with many Australian, New Zealand, and French troops, attempted to knock Turkey out of the war** by invading the Gallipoli Peninsula near the Turkish capital in 1915. The effort was a total failure.

729. **Winston Churchill came up with the idea and was blamed for what happened**. Later studies have shown that though the Allies likely would have lost the battle, **Churchill was not the only one who deserved blame** for it.

730. **During most of the war, the British supreme army commander was General Douglas Haig,** who came to represent all that was wrong about the British officer corps. **Haig and his staff did not seem to care about the number of casualties and kept using the same tactics** almost until the war's end.

731. **One of the officers opposing the Allies at Gallipoli was Mustafa Kemal**, who became **the first president of the Turkish Republic in 1918** when the Ottoman Empire fell. He is known as **Ataturk, "Father of the Turks."**

732. **Submarines had been used in the US Civil War**, but they were often more dangerous to the men in them than to anyone else. **WWI saw the use of the first "modern" and deadly submarines in warfare.**

733. **German U-boats attempted to disrupt Allied supply lines** carrying raw materials needed for industrial production. This caused shortages that affected civilians in Britain, France, and other nations. **Britain was particularly vulnerable since much of its food came from overseas.**

The New York Times.

ITANIA SUNK BY A SUBMARINE, PROBABLY 1,260 DEAD;
VICE TORPEDOED OFF IRISH COAST; SINKS IN 15 MINUTES
CAPT. TURNER SAVED, FROHMAN AND VANDERBILT MISSIN
WASHINGTON BELIEVES THAT A GRAVE CRISIS IS AT HA

The Lost Cunard Steamship Lusitania

734. **In 1915, a German U-boat sunk the passenger ship *Lusitania*, which killed almost 1,200 passengers aboard. Over a hundred of them were American citizens.** Germany claimed the British liner was carrying weapons and war supplies, which the English denied. **Decades later, it was proved that over 170 tons of shells and bullets were on board.**

735. **British naval forces implemented a blockade on German ports** that lasted throughout WWI. **This almost completely halted Germany's imports and exports**, causing severe shortages and leading to famine and malnutrition among its civilians.

736. **In 1916, British forces launched the Battle of Jutland**, a massive naval confrontation that was both tactically inconclusive and strategically indecisive. **The battle led to significant losses on both sides.**

737. **Though the Battle of Jutland was a stalemate, the British lost more ships than the Germans**. However, the British had more to lose. The German surface fleet did not engage in any other important battles during the war.

738. **In 1916, the British lost over thirty thousand men killed and wounded *in one day* at the Battle of the Somme**, which has been memorialized in English poems and stories.

739. Many famous works came from WWI. **Siegfried Sassoon is known for his sarcastic view on patriotism.** Perhaps the most famous work was **"In Flanders Fields" by Canadian army surgeon John McCrae.**

740. **In 1917, Russia was forced out of World War I after a bloody revolution led by Vladimir Lenin** overthrew **Tsar Nicholas II's government**.

741. **On April 6th, 1917, America declared war on Germany**, joining the Allied war effort.

742. **Great Britain had to borrow enormous sums of money from the United States to keep fighting the war**, which was one of the many things that contributed to the Great Depression.

743. **The British army was the first to use mass formations of tanks**. This happened near **the French town of Cambrai** in late 1917. Tanks broke through enemy lines without taking heavy losses from artillery fire.

744. **WWI brought about significant advancements in technology, such as tanks, airplanes, machine guns, and chemical weapons**. The effects of chemical weapons were horrible, causing external and internal burns and internal fluid buildup in the lungs that could drown a person. **After the war, most nations signed various agreements, promising not to use chemical weapons ever again.**

745. **Because both sides dug strong defensive trenches and fortifications on the Western Front,** specific weapons were created to help attackers. One was **the submachine gun**, and the other was **the terrifying flamethrower**.

746. **Depending on the model, flamethrowers could squirt a hot jet of flame many yards**. Men were so terrified of being set on fire that the men who carried the flamethrowers were "high-value targets" in any assault.

747. The RFC, **the "Royal Flying Corps," was the British air force during WWI.** Planes were used in combat for the first time during the war.

748. **English cities were bombed by German bombers and Zeppelins during the war.** Though these raids did far less damage than what occurred in WWII, they made **the English realize they were vulnerable to foreign attacks from the skies.**

749. **WWI saw the first use of aircraft carriers**, but their use was very limited. It would not be **until WWII that aircraft carriers would become critical at sea**.

750. **In 1917, Allied forces led by General Edmund Allenby captured Jerusalem from Turkish forces**. Jerusalem had been under Muslim rule for four centuries. This event marked an **important milestone in WWI's Middle Eastern campaign**. It also had a **profound effect on the Middle East** since much of the area was controlled by Europeans after the war.

751. **In January 1918, US President Woodrow Wilson issued his famous Fourteen Points speech,** outlining his vision for peace following the Great War. His speech would eventually lead to the establishment of **the League of Nations in 1920**. This organization wanted to promote international cooperation and prevent further wars.

752. **The fighting ended at 11 a.m. on November 11th, 1918.** This was due to the armistice or ceasefire that both sides agreed to. However, it was clear to most people on both sides that the Central Powers, specifically **Germany, had lost the war.**

753. **WWI saw some major advances in medical science. Antibiotics were used** to treat wounded soldiers and **help prevent infections from spreading**. These drugs would eventually become essential components of modern healthcare, saving countless lives worldwide.

754. **In 1918, the Spanish flu epidemic killed an estimated fifty million people** around the world. **More people died of the Spanish flu than from the war!**

755. **The Treaty of Versailles was signed on June 28th, 1919, marking the official end of WWI.**

756. **The Treaty of Versailles severely weakened Germany by forcing it to surrender its colonies and pay huge reparations**. The Germans resented the treaty. They would later lend their support to a group that promised to bring back the Germany of old. **This group was the Nazi Party.**

757. **The British prime minister at the end of the war was David Lloyd-George,** the first of four Welsh-born prime ministers in British history and one of the authors of the Treaty of Versailles.

758. **Millions of people died during WWI. British losses are estimated at over 700,000 men from the British Isles.** That number rises to around one million when Britain's possessions are taken into account.

759. **The Britons, especially the Englishmen, killed during the war came to be known as the "Lost Generation."**

760. **Because of the almost unending shelling on the Western Front, many men, including thousands of British soldiers, developed PTSD** (post-traumatic stress disorder). Back then, it was called **"shell shock"** and often showed itself through uncontrollable shaking, spasms, and panic.

The Women's Suffrage Movement

Today, many women take it for granted that they can vote in important elections and have a voice in their government, but **the right to vote in Britain did not come easy.** Another name for voting is **"suffrage,"** and the **women and men who fought for the women's right to vote were subjected to harassment, jail, beatings,** and other mistreatment at the hands of authorities and conservative forces. Let's examine twenty important facts about this movement.

761. **The women's suffrage movement in Great Britain aimed to secure voting rights for women,** allowing them to participate in the democratic process.

762. **The movement began in the mid-19th century with the formation of various organizations, such as the National Society for Women's Suffrage** (1867) and **the Women's Social and Political Union** (1903).

763. One of the prominent figures in the suffrage movement was **Emmeline Pankhurst,** who, along **with her daughters Christabel and Sylvia,** founded **the Women's Social and Political Union** (WSPU).

764. **The WSPU adopted more militant and aggressive tactics in their fight for suffrage.**

765. **The suffrage movement faced opposition from men and women who believed that a woman's place was in the home** and that they were unfit to participate in politics.

766. **Various methods were employed by suffragettes to gain attention** and advocate for their cause. These methods included **protests, hunger strikes, and acts of civil disobedience like blocking the entrances to important government buildings.**

767. **The suffrage movement faced significant setbacks.** Many suffragettes were arrested and imprisoned for their actions. They were often subjected to harsh treatment while in prison.

768. **One of the most famous tactics the suffragettes used in prison was the hunger strike,** in which they refused to eat.

769. **Rather than be blamed for allowing these women to die from hunger, the authorities often force-fed them, which was painful and torturous**.

770. **The suffrage movement gained momentum during World War I when women took on roles traditionally held by men**, such as **working in factories and serving in the armed forces.** This helped to change public opinion regarding women's capabilities.

771. **The Representation of the People Act of 1918 granted voting rights to women over the age of thirty** who met certain property qualifications. This marked a significant milestone for the suffrage movement.

772. **The 1918 act was also the first time almost all adult men were able to vote.**

773. **The Equal Franchise Act of 1928 extended voting rights to all women over the age of twenty-one**, putting them on equal footing with men.

774. **The suffrage movement in Great Britain inspired similar movements in other countries around the world,** including the United States, Canada, Australia, and New Zealand.

775. **Many suffragettes faced public ridicule and were labeled as radicals** or troublemakers for their involvement in the movement.

776. **Many also questioned their sexuality** at a time when same-sex relationships were severely looked down on and sometimes prosecuted.

777. **The suffrage movement brought together women from various social and economic backgrounds**, including working-class women, middle-class women, and even some members of the aristocracy.

778. **One of the men who opposed women's suffrage but later admitted he was wrong was Winston Churchill.** He was a member of Parliament and a member of the Cabinet at times during the suffragettes' struggle.

779. **Notable suffragettes like Emily Davison sacrificed their lives for the cause. Emily Davison died after throwing herself in front of the king's horse during the 1913 Epsom Derby**. Like many other suffragettes, she had gone on numerous hunger strikes and had been arrested a number of times for her beliefs.

780. **The suffrage movement in Great Britain paved the way for future advancements in women's rights,** leading to greater gender equality in various aspects of society today.

The General Strike

(1926)

The UK General Strike of 1926 was a nine-day work strike. Over 1.7 million workers took part in it. This strike **aimed at forcing the government** to intervene **in preventing wage reductions and worsening conditions for coal miners.** The strike had many supporters, including labor activists, **the Labour Party**, and even **the Communist Party of Great Britain**. The strike is remembered as a significant example of **workers' actions to secure better working conditions.** Let's look at ten interesting facts about **the General Strike.**

781. **The General Strike of 1926 was a nine-day event that started on May 4th and occurred in much of the United Kingdom.**

782. **It was organized by coal miner unions to protest** wage cuts and poor working conditions.

783. **The coal miners had support from many different industrial sectors**, including miners, transport workers, printers, and dockworkers.

784. **More than three million people participated**, making it one of the largest strikes in history and the first of its kind in England.

785. **Prime Minister Stanley Baldwin called an emergency meeting of Parliament**, where he made proposals like raising wages. However, the proposals did not pass, as his ideas did not go far enough for the strikers.

786. **After nine days of striking, the government brought in troops to break up picket lines so they could get supplies into some cities like London**. Some of the strikers were dockworkers and people who worked on the canals and railways. These people were needed to supply the city.

787. **Despite its large size, only minimal violence occurred during the strike**. Most of the **violence was caused by police action against protesters** or strikers attacking property or businesses deemed as **"scab" operations** (those who continued to operate despite being asked not to).

788. Oddly enough, **King George V agreed with many of the miners' demands**, but he did not have the power to do anything about the strike. He famously said to anti-strike politicians, **"Try living on their wages before you judge them."**

789. **Chancellor of the Exchequer Winston Churchill was very much against the strike** and urged **Prime Minister Stanley Baldwin** to take forceful action. **Baldwin refused,** and the strike ended in a relatively peaceful manner.

790. **Eventually, negotiations between employers and union leaders led to both sides agreeing on some improvements**, such as setting minimum wages and reducing the number of hours worked per week. The union leaders made little progress on pay increases.

The Great Depression

(1929–1939)

The Great Depression was a worldwide economic collapse that hit the industrialized countries of Europe and North America particularly hard. The Depression had many causes, some of which were rooted in **WWI and rampant speculation of stocks**. The spark that set off **the Great Depression began in New York and spread quickly through the industrialized world,** causing untold suffering and the rise of authoritarianism in Europe. Let's look at twenty facts about this important moment in history.

791. **The Depression began when the New York Stock Exchange began a series of steep drops from October 24th to October 29th**. October 29th is generally considered the day of **the Great Wall Street Crash of 1929**. The stock market lost more than half its value.

792. **In both the UK and the US, people could buy stocks "on margin," meaning they would be loaned money to buy stocks**. They would have to pay the loan when the stock went up. When the stock went down, they would have to pay their loan and any loss taken.

793. **Many people bought stocks on margin**. But when banks called in their margins, very few people could pay them back, leading to bank failures.

794. **Many company shares became worthless**. Many owners owned stock in their businesses. **Thousands of companies went out of business in the US, the UK**, and throughout the world.

795. **Since so many people lost money**, there was little money left over to invest. **Many companies that depended on investments could no longer afford to keep paying all their workers.** The industrial areas, such as **coal mining and transportation**, were hit the hardest.

796. **The slowdown in the economy meant people were eating less, which affected farming**. The disappearance of farms contributed to hunger around the globe, including in **Great Britain**.

797. Though **the Great Depression** began with **the New York Wall Street Crash**, **the Depression in Great Britain** didn't get bad until some months later.

798. **Though there had been economic depressions in Britain and the US before**, they were mild and short-lived in comparison to **the Great Depression**.

799. Before the Depression began, **Britain and much of Europe had begun to import many American goods.** Britain was a **net exporter**, meaning it sold more than it bought overseas.

800. **During the Depression, American exports to Europe greatly decreased**, which affected the economy. Britain also sold its goods around the world, but people couldn't afford to buy them, **which caused the British economy to worsen.**

801. **Twenty percent of the working population in the UK was unemployed in 1933**, the highest it had ever been. **More than three million people did not have a job.**

802. **The UK had unemployment insurance in 1911**, long before the US, which introduced it in 1932.

803. **Big industrial areas like Liverpool and southern Wales experienced higher unemployment than the rest of the country**, reaching close to one in three people over eighteen years old (around 33 percent).

804. **Crime in Great Britain increased during the Depression.**

805. **The aristocracy and upper middle class in England were worried that the lingering Depression might cause a revolution**. In Germany, **Hitler took power in early 1933**. In other European countries, extreme left- and right-wing movements began.

806. **Oswald Mosley, an upper-class former member of Parliament, started the British Union of Fascists in 1932**. He visited **fascist Italy and Nazi Germany** to look for support.
807. **Mosley's party never enjoyed great popularity**, but many supporters lived in London, making the party seem larger than it was. **Mosley was jailed in 1940 for treason and spent all of WWII in prison.**

808. **In 1931, the government began a series of banking, business, and economic reforms that would slowly begin the nation's recovery from the Depression.**
809. **Unfortunately for the UK, the Depression was not fully over when WWII began in September 1939.**

810. **After WWII, a variety of factors, including the immense debt Great Britain gained from borrowing billions from the US during the war**, caused the 1940s to be a time of continued economic suffering for many people.

World War II

(1939–1945)

World War II was a global conflict that resulted in more than eighty million deaths worldwide. We'll learn forty interesting facts about the people and events that shaped the war, from **the Allied Powers** (led by the United States, the United Kingdom, the Soviet Union, France, and China) to **the Axis Powers** (led by Germany, Italy, and Japan). **Strategies and advanced weapons were key to winning the war.** We will also explore the losses suffered by each side and **the important role women played in the war** effort.

811. **Adolf Hitler became the leader of Germany in 1933.**

812. **Nazi Germany was responsible for starting World War II in Europe** when it invaded Poland on September 1st, 1939.

813. **In May 1940, Hitler invaded western Europe, conquering France, Belgium, and Holland.** British troops were forced to retreat into a pocket around the French port of Dunkirk.

814. **Around 850 private boats sailed to Dunkirk to help rescue the soldiers trapped there.** The navy also arrived to help in the rescue effort. **Dunkirk is one of the greatest stories of the war.**

815. **The Royal Navy still dominated the waters, especially near Europe and the Middle East.** Part of **the reason Italy joined Hitler was because it wanted to gain control of the Mediterranean and the Suez Canal**. On paper, Italy had a very strong navy.

816. **At the same time Hitler was invading France, Winston Churchill became prime minister of Britain.**

817. Many people doubted that anyone could handle the prime minister's job during this intense time in history. However, **Churchill rose to the occasion, creating the position of minister of defense.**

818. **Churchill had the idea for commando troops** (what we call "special forces" today) because **he had been captured by a special Boer unit called *Kommandos*.**

819. **The commandos staged raids along the coasts of Europe, hoping to cause Hitler to spread his forces to defend the long coastline.** They also worked to gain intelligence and give hope to people in the UK and Europe.

820. **The Battle of Britain in 1940 was Germany's attempt to dominate the skies over the English Channel** and the southern coast of England. Germany wanted to invade the country.

821. **Despite the greater number of German planes, the British RAF ("Royal Air Force") enjoyed many advantages**, like the earlier development of radar. British planes were also able to use less fuel than the Germans because they were flying over their homeland.

822. **The famous fighter pilot heroes of the RAF were known as "the Few" from a speech by Churchill**, where he thanked them for their service and sacrifice.

823. **During the war, women took over jobs that had previously been done by men**. Many men fought in the war, leaving jobs open that needed to be filled. Women produced weapons or other necessities for the country's war effort.

824. **During World War II, many countries experienced food shortages due to rationing**. Rationing meant people had limited access to certain items, such as sugar, butter, and coffee. However, the people could still get enough sustenance thanks to programs like **Britain's "Dig for Victory" campaign**, which encouraged citizens to grow their own vegetables at home.

825. **Britain depended on oil from Asia and the Middle East** for its war effort. Therefore, they sent large armies, planes, and many ships to those areas to defend them. **There were more British soldiers overseas than there were defending Britain itself.**

826. **Italian troops in North Africa were defeated by the British, forcing Hitler to intervene there. In 1941**, he sent one of his best **generals, Erwin Rommel**, with tanks and infantry to face the British. **Rommel's force was called the Afrika Korps**.

827. For almost two years, **the British and Germans fought across much of North Africa**. The turning point in the battle was **the British victory at El-Alamein in Egypt.**

828. **In June 1941, Hitler invaded the Soviet Union** (the USSR). This was the largest invasion in history. **Overnight, the USSR went from being a nation that Britain treated with suspicion to an ally**. While the UK was experiencing its own troubles, the British sent many war supplies to the USSR.

829. **The Germans had developed a complex code machine in 1926 that they believed was unbreakable. The Enigma machine** allowed German commanders to communicate without fear of enemies translating their messages, leading to some significant victories.

830. **To combat the Enigma machine, British codebreakers deciphered its secrets in 1941, using an advanced machine developed at Bletchley Park in England known as Colossus.** This machine could decode messages quickly enough to give valuable intelligence about troop or submarine movements so England could plan for an attack ahead of time!

831. **Hitler was an ally of Japan**. When the **Japanese attacked the US Navy at Pearl Harbor,** Hawaii, in late 1941, **Hitler declared war on the US.**

832. **At the same time Japan was attacking Pearl Harbor, the Japanese attacked British, American, and Dutch colonies in Asia. Singapore, Malaya, Hong Kong, and Burma** were all attacked. Only part of Burma remained British.

833. **The Dutch East Indies were conquered by the Japanese** as well. **The Philippines** and **the islands of Wake and Guam** were also taken by the Japanese.

834. **By the time the US entered the war, the US had been supplying Britain with war equipment, food, and much else**. The Americans helped the British defend their supply routes at sea and **fought the Germans in Africa**.

835. **In November 1942, US troops landed in western North Africa, pushing the Germans and their allies eastward**. Meanwhile, the British pushed the Germans westward. In the summer of 1943, the Germans and Italians retreated from North Africa to defend Italy.

836. **In 1943, US and British forces conquered the Italian island of Sicily and then invaded Italy itself.** Generally speaking, the British moved up the east coast of Italy while the Americans moved up the west coast.

837. **The Italian campaign was Churchill's idea**. He hoped Allied troops could move through Italy into southern Germany. **It was a bad idea** for many reasons. At the end of the war, Allied troops were still fighting in Italy.

838. **The Battle of Monte Cassino** took place from January 17th to May 18th, 1944. Allied forces **managed to break through German lines** after a months-long siege. **This battle is considered to be one of the bloodiest battles during WWII,** with over fifty-five thousand Allied casualties and an estimated twenty thousand for the Germans.

839. **By the time Rome was conquered in June 1944, it was clear that Britain was taking a backseat in the war.** The US was supplying more men, equipment, and money to the war effort than Britain. With some exceptions, the British had to go along with the Americans' ideas for the rest of the war.

840. On June 6th, 1944, **Allied troops traveled from England to Normandy, France, in the D-Day invasion.** D-Day was the beginning of the Allied attempt to liberate northwestern Europe.

841. **At about the same time as D-Day, the British were fighting off Japanese attacks in Burma** and the eastern border of India.

842. **Though British and Imperial forces** (mostly Australia, New Zealand, and India) fought in the Pacific, **the larger British effort was against the Nazis in Europe**. The Nazis presented a greater threat to England itself.

843. **Many refugees from Nazi-dominated Europe fled to England**. Many of them formed army, commando, and air force units to help regain their homelands. **Many of the Imperial troops fighting in Europe were New Zealanders, Canadians, and Indians.**

844. *Another group of refugees, some of them German Jews,* knew what life was like in Germany and occupied Europe. **They became spies or intelligence agents during the war.**

845. The most famous of **the resistance movements based in England was the French Resistance**, led by future French president and WWI hero **Charles de Gaulle**.

846. **By the spring of 1945, Hitler had been defeated**. Germany and Berlin, its capital, were divided into four zones of control. **The US, the UK, France, and the USSR took control of the four zones. The British sector was in the northeast**, and the British sector of Berlin was between the French in the north and the Americans in the south.

847. **British territories were restored to British control with the surrender of Japan in the late summer of 1945**. Within a few short years, many of these territories would be fighting against the British to achieve their independence.

848. **Over eighty million people died during WWII, making it one of the deadliest wars in history.** While Britain suffered economic and personal losses, **it suffered only around 450,000 deaths in the war.** Other countries had a much higher death count.

849. **Though WWI had weakened Great Britain, it was still considered one of the strongest countries on Earth.** When WWII ended, everyone knew that **Britain's time as a world superpower was over.**

850. **Most historians agree that had Britain not held out against Hitler in 1940, the war might have ended in a negotiated peace** that left Hitler in command of all of Europe. It is also plausible the war would have continued for many more years.

The Welfare State

(1946–1979)

Before WWII ended, the British people voted Winston Churchill out of office, despite having great respect for him. **They saw him as a great war leader, but they believed he was too conservative to deal with the changes many people wanted** to take place in the UK. After WWII, **the British government implemented social reforms that came to collectively be called the Welfare State**. This system's goal was to provide economic security and social welfare services to citizens in England, Scotland, Wales, and Northern Ireland.

Despite a sharp shift away from **the Welfare State in 1979**, the changes implemented within this new system were seen as a major step forward for social justice. **The changes provided a safety net for people in need,** reduced poverty and inequality, and improved living standards for the citizens. Let's look at twenty interesting facts about **the Welfare State.**

851. **The Welfare State was a period of social reform in the United Kingdom** between 1946 and 1979. It started under **Labour Prime Minister Clement Attlee** in 1946.

852. During this period, **the government created measures to improve public services and social security**, such as **the National Health Service** (NHS).

853. **Under the Welfare State, unemployment benefits were expanded**. National insurance was introduced to provide protection against illness and poverty in old age.

854. **Government subsidies for food, fuel, and rent** were also introduced during this period. Other reforms included measures to tackle discrimination based on race and gender.

855. **The government gradually increased spending on public services**, such as health care, education, and housing.

856. **Public education became free at all levels up to the university** level under the 1944 Education Act. Don't be confused, though. To this day, **private schools and academies in Great Britain are called "public schools."**

857. **The 1944 Education Act** made it easier for girls and children of working-class families to attend school.

858. **Housing subsidy schemes were set up to help people buy their own homes** or rent properties at affordable rates. **Construction of housing projects called "council homes"** or **"council tenancies"** began in most British cities as a way to provide affordable housing.

859. **Many famous British rock bands** in the 1960s and 1970s sang about how bad life in council projects really was.

860. In 1948, **Britain launched the National Health Service** (NHS), which provided universal healthcare. Medical treatments were funded by taxation rather than individual payments.

861. For a time **after the war, prescriptions were free of charge**, but for a variety of reasons, including a change of government, **fees began to be charged** for most prescription drugs.

862. In 1952, **London was affected by the Great Smog, a cloud of thick pollution**. The 1956 **Clean Air Act regulated smoke emissions** from industrial buildings. New laws regarding clean water supplies were introduced in 1961.

863. **The 1959 Mental Health Act provided more rights to people with mental health problems.** The 1967 Abortion Act made abortion legal under certain conditions.

864. **The 1968 Trade Union Reform Bill** allowed trade unions greater freedom from state control, allowing them to negotiate pay raises for their members.

865. **From 1969 onward, comprehensive education was implemented across Britain,** which provided equal access to education for all children regardless of their ability or racial or economic background.

866. **The 1971 Industrial Relations Act protected workers' rights** by providing legal recognition for trade unions and introducing guidelines about working hours and severance pay.

867. **During this time, British people developed a reputation for bad teeth**. This was partially due to the fact that two of the cheapest commodities in post-war Britain were sugar and flour. **Lots of bread, jam, and sugar meant lots of cavities.**

868. During this period**, there were also measures taken to reduce poverty**, including the introduction of a national minimum wage.

869. **Many of these laws and schemes were more effective on paper than in reality**. Bureaucratic **"red tape"** (meaning unnecessary rules, paperwork, and lack of direction) slowed progress or made the changes ineffective.

870. Despite expanding the government's role in everyday life, **it was difficult for the British to recover from WWII.** They owed a great deal of money. Many men had been killed or injured. **And there was great damage from German bombing raids**. For many in Britain, the post-war years were harder economically than the war years.

The Suez Crisis

(1956)

The Suez Crisis was a major international event that shaped global politics for decades to come. We'll discover **the political and military actions** of the major players involved and **the UN's role in resolving some of the event's** lasting economic and political impacts. Discover ten capitating facts about this moment in history.

871. **The Suez Canal was built in 1869 by French engineer Ferdinand de Lesseps**. It was completed in 1875.

872. **The Suez Crisis happened in 1956**. It was a conflict between **Egypt and Israel**, the latter of which had just become a new country.

873. **At the time of the crisis, the canal was owned by the Suez Canal Company, a private company based in Britain and France.**

874. **The Suez Crisis was a major international issue that involved many different countries, including the United States, the United Kingdom, France, and the Soviet Union**.

875. **Problems began when Egypt nationalized the Suez Canal, which was a vital shipping route between the Mediterranean and the Red Sea.**

876. This move was seen as an act of aggression by Israel. **Israel invaded Egypt because of it.**

877. **British and French forces took control of the Suez Canal**, which both nations depended on for supplies from the Middle East and Asia.

878. **The crisis had far-reaching effects, including strengthening the United Nations as a peacekeeping force**, the rise of Arab nationalism, and the weakening of European powers. It also led to **the United States and the Soviet Union becoming more involved in the affairs of the Middle East.**

879. For a variety of reasons, including **serious threats made by the Soviet Union over British and French** possession of the canal, **the US put pressure on both countries to remove their troops from the canal zone.** Many historians see Britain's and France's agreement with American demands as yet another sign of these nations' decline in power and influence.

880. **The Suez Canal is still a major waterway today**. It is one of the busiest shipping routes in the world.

Decolonization

(1947–1966)

Britain's complex process of decolonization took place in the mid-20th century. Many countries that had been **ruled by Great Britain gained independence**. Discover how **decolonization ultimately changed** the face of the world with these fifteen interesting facts.

881. **Decolonization is the process of freeing countries from the control of colonial powers.** It occurred mainly in the mid-20th century, although some countries were freed later. For instance, **Britain finally gave control of Hong Kong back to China in 1997.**

882. **Though imperialism/colonization meant that people were often treated as second-class citizens**, it also meant the people were protected by a stronger power.

883. **Decolonization took place mainly in Asia and Africa.**

884. **Many countries experienced civil unrest during decolonization.** Violent protests and revolts occurred in some areas.

885. **The most prominent country to gain independence during decolonization was India** in 1947.

886. **India was the largest country to gain independence from Britain during decolonization**, though it was later divided into two countries: **India and Pakistan**. Pakistan later split in two, with a new country called **Bangladesh** emerging in 1971.

887. Probably the most famous figure of the decolonization period was **Mahatma Gandhi, an Indian lawyer** who preached a policy of non-violent protest that likely prevented much bloodshed before **India gained independence**. Gandhi influenced many other activists, including **Martin Luther King Jr**. in the United States.

888. **The Mau Mau Rebellion took place in Kenya** from 1952 to 1960. Though the rebellion was eventually defeated and resulted in widespread brutality on both sides, Kenya became an independent nation in 1963.

889. Some of the other African countries that gained **independence from Britain include Zimbabwe, Namibia, Gambia, and Cameroon.**

890. In 1956, the first big wave of decolonization began with **the independence of Sudan and Malaysia from Great Britain.**

891. By the early 1970s, the British Empire was a shell of what it had been. The British Commonwealth was formed. **The British Commonwealth contains the former British colonies and territories closely linked with the United Kingdom.**

892. Between 1979 and 1990, the **UK gave independence to Belize, Dominica, Kiribati, the Solomon Islands, St. Lucia, St. Vincent and the Grenadines, and Vanuatu.**

893. **At the British Empire's height in the early 20th century, it consisted of fifty-seven territories**. Most of them are now independent. Today, there are **fourteen overseas territories that are British possessions,** though most of them have a great deal of independence.

894. **Though European and British imperialism was unfair and oppressive in many ways, there were a number of developments that benefited the people**, such as modern infrastructure and modern educational systems.

895. **In 2023, there are still fourteen British Overseas Territories**. Most are small islands in the Atlantic, but there are two in the Pacific and the British Antarctic Territory.

British Culture after WWII: Music, Movies, and More

Throughout WWI and into the 1940s, American culture had a great impact on British popular culture. In this section, you'll learn more about how it spread and how the **British made rock music their own in the 1960s**. You'll also find out about famous British actors, movies, and TV shows!

896. **With the invention of the radio and the worldwide distribution of newspapers, the world became closer than ever.** For Britain, that meant new ideas in fashion, music, and other art forms.

897. **Before WWI, much of the entertainment in the UK had originated there**, but with radio and **the huge numbers of American** troops in **England** and **France** during **WWI, American music** and culture **spread throughout western Europe**.

898. **The first wave of American music to capture the hearts of the English was jazz.** Many British jazz bands emerged during this time. They toured the country, mostly **playing American songs** and using American slang in their lyrics.

899. **Jazz music has roots in African American culture**, giving the British their first real taste of African American culture.

900. **Many African American musicians moved to England** and other parts of western Europe, where discrimination against them was much less common. However, it still existed.

901. **In the 1930s and 1940s, a new kind of music called swing became popular**. Swing music was faster and more organized. It was very fun to dance to.

902. **American music and movies ushered in a new age of fashion in Britain**, especially in England. Not all Britons approved of the changes. **Just like in America, many older and conservative people believed jazz and swing music led to sexual activity, drug use,** excessive drinking, revealing fashion, and more.

903. **By the late 1920s, England had its own thriving movie industry**. British movies were shown around the world, especially in the territories **of the British Empire**.

904. **Many British actors became famous in the United States**. Some were regarded as better actors than Americans. **Many British actors had trained on the stage**, performing **Shakespeare** and **other classic plays**.

905. **Laurence Olivier is considered by many to be the best actor of the 20th century**. He starred in British and American productions.

906. **One of the first popular color movies was the American Civil War epic, *Gone with the Wind*,** which was released in December 1939. Many people don't know that three of its main actors were British: Vivien Leigh, Leslie Howard, and Olivia de Havilland.

907. **Before WWII, some of the most popular plays on Broadway were written by English playwright Noel Coward**.

908. **During WWII, millions of Americans came to England to prepare for the invasion of France.** They influenced many young people with their dress, **chewing gum** (which was new to England), **music, and slang.**

909. **In the early 1950s, rock and roll came to Britain from America, causing a craze among the British youth who listened to it on the radio.** They bought albums imported from America.

910. **Four Englishman who fell in love with American music at this time were John Lennon, Paul McCartney, George Harrison, and Richard Starkey** (better known as Ringo Starr). These men would be part of **the Beatles**, which is perhaps the most popular rock band of all time.

911. **Music from Jamaica, a British territory, also became popular at this time**. Rock steady, ska, and reggae music became very popular in the UK, especially among many British ethnic groups.

912. **In 1962 and 1963, Beatlemania took over England and Scotland and then spread to Europe,** British Overseas Territories, Canada, Australia, and the United States. **Hundreds of thousands of people clogged the streets and arrived at airports to see the Beatles**.

913. **The Beatles set off a frenzy for any rock music coming from England**. **The Rolling Stones, the Who, the Kinks, and Led Zeppelin** were just four of the many groups and artists that were part of what people in America called the British Invasion.

914. **Rock musicians protested a lot of what they saw going on around them in the 1960s and early 1970s**. By the mid-1970s, it seemed like popular music ignored the problems of suburban life and life in the inner cities, especially in the English-speaking world.

915. **Because of this, punk rock began in the late 1970s in both the UK and the US**. Punk rock music and fashion and the outrageous behavior that went with the genre shocked many people. Though there were many influential British punk rock groups, the most famous was the Sex Pistols.

916. **One of the Sex Pistols' most popular songs was "God Save the Queen."** This song **heavily criticized Queen Elizabeth and the British government and aristocracy**. The song and the album it was on were banned from the radio. However, **the record sold more than any other in England that year.**

917. **New wave began in the UK and the US out of some of the changes happening in music and technology**. Many British new wave groups, like **Depeche Mode, Echo and the Bunnymen, and the Cure**, became immensely popular in Britain and the US.

918. **In the 1990s and 2000s, many English movies became popular around the world.** Some of these include ***About a Boy*, *Notting Hill*, *Bridget Jones's Diary*, and *Snatch*.**

919. **The depictions of aristocratic life in Britain became popular in the 1990s and 2010s with movies and television shows like *Remains of the Day* and *Downton Abbey*.**

920. In the 1970s, **popular British comedies, like the low-brow *Benny Hill Show*** or the hilarious but strange ***Monty Python's Flying Circus***, became huge hits in the US.

The Thatcher Years

(1979–1990)

The Thatcher Years were a time of great change and reform in Great Britain. This period of time is named **for Prime Minister Margaret Thatcher**, the first female prime minister. Her nickname was the **"Iron Lady"** for her toughness and determination. **"Thatcherism" sought to reduce the role of the state, privatize nationalized industries, and deregulate the economy.** Let's learn twenty facts about the many changes during Thatcher's time as prime minister.

921. **Margaret Thatcher came from the Conservative Party.** She became **the first female prime minister of Great Britain** on May 4th, 1979.

922. **Thatcher and the Conservative Party were determined to roll back many of the state-funded programs that had begun in the post-WWII years.** They believed these programs stifled free enterprise and cost the government too much money.

923. **In 1981, Americans had a conservative in charge, Ronald Reagan. Reagan and Thatcher believed in many of the same things**, including the need to stand up more strongly to **the Soviet Union**. The Soviet Union had become more active by 1980, attempting to spread communist ideology.

924. During this period, **British and American governments worked to weaken Soviet control of Eastern Europe,** beginning with Poland.

925. **The British Nationality Act of 1981** was passed during the Thatcher Years, which allowed citizens of British Commonwealth countries to have the same rights as British citizens.

926. **The Thatcher Years saw an increase in immigration to the UK**, with people from Asia, Africa, and the Caribbean coming to live and work in the UK.

927. **On April 2nd, 1982, Argentina invaded the Falkland Islands, a British possession off the coast of Argentina**. The Argentines believed the islands belonged to them, but Britain disagreed. From April to June, Argentina and the UK fought a war over the islands. The British won.

928. **The Thatcher Years saw the signing of the Anglo-Irish Agreement in 1985**, which established a relationship between **the UK and the Republic of Ireland**, the southern independent part of the island.

929. **The Thatcher Years saw the beginning of the building of the Channel Tunnel,** a rail tunnel connecting England with France.

930. **The Thatcher Years also saw the introduction of the Environment Act**, which set out regulations to protect the environment.

931. **The Thatcher Years saw the introduction of the national curriculum**, which standardized education across the UK.

932. During the Thatcher Years, **the UK helped to create the Single European Act**, which aimed to create a single European currency by 1997. The euro came about because of this act.

933. **The Thatcher Years saw the privatization of many public services and industries,** including British Rail and British Telecom.

934. **The Thatcher Years saw the introduction of the poll tax,** which was a flat-rate tax on each person in the UK.

935. **The Thatcher Years also saw the introduction of the right to buy council houses,** which were apartment and housing project units people could rent relatively cheaply. These changes allowed people to buy homes with generally favorable terms.

936. **In 1984, the Police and Criminal Evidence Act was passed**. It set out regulations for the police to follow when dealing with criminal matters.

937. **By the end of the Thatcher Years, the UK saw a decrease in unemployment and a rise in living standards.** However, for much of the Thatcher era, unemployment, poverty, and crime were high in the inner cities.

938. **Younger people in Britain were divided on Thatcher's leadership**. Many in the cities believed she did not care for the poor. The upper-middle class and the people living outside the cities saw her as the person who could restore Britain's economic power and influence.

939. **After eleven years in power, Margaret Thatcher lost a vote of support in the Conservative Party,** leading to her resignation and the eventual election of the next prime minister, **Conservative Party member John Major.**

940. **Thatcher and her legacy are still hated by many in the UK**, especially among the poor, minorities, and liberals.

The Falklands War

(1982)

The Falklands War was a conflict between Argentina and the United Kingdom, lasting from April to June of 1982. **Why did Argentina invade the British-controlled Falkland Islands?** How did a **British naval force retake the islands?** Learn about **the battles fought during the war** and the long-term effects on **Britain and Argentina** with these twenty enthralling facts.

941. **The Falklands War was a conflict between Argentina and the United Kingdom** that took place from April to June of 1982. It was the first war fought in **the South Atlantic** since World War II.

942. **The Falkland Islands are a group of islands in the South Atlantic Ocean** located about 930 miles off the east coast of Argentina.

943. **The Falkland Islands had been under British control since 1833.**

944. **Argentina had wanted to take control of the islands** for many years before the war began.

945. **Argentina's invasion of the British-controlled Falkland Islands began on April 2nd, 1982.**

946. **Argentina claimed the islands were theirs and had previously named the islands the Malvinas.**

947. **The British government ordered a naval task force to the South Atlantic Ocean to take back the islands.**

948. Many important battles were fought during the war, including **the Battle of San Carlos Water, the Battle of Goose Green, and the Battle of Mount Harriet.**

949. On May 21st, 1982, a British submarine sank the Argentine cruiser *General Belgrano*. This marked the largest loss of life in a single day of the war.

950. **Argentina surrendered on June 14th, 1982**, and the British regained control of the islands.

951. **The war was the first British victory in an overseas conflict since the end of World War II.**

952. **The British lost 255 men. The Argentinians lost 649**. Three Falkland Islanders and a British civilian also lost their lives during the war.

953. **The British took most of the Argentinian occupation forces prisoner by the end of the war.** They captured over eleven thousand men, all of whom were released when the war ended.

954. **Behind the scenes, the United States, Britain's closest ally, warned other powers, namely the Soviet Union,** from becoming involved in the conflict.

955. **Many people criticized the British government for its decision to send troops to the Falkland Islands instead of trying to find a diplomatic solution.** However, an equal number of people criticized Argentina for invading the islands in the first place.

956. **The war caused tensions between Argentina and the United Kingdom that still exist today.**

957. **The war was an important factor in the British general election of 1983, which returned Thatcher to power.**

958. **The war was expensive for both sides, but Great Britain could afford the cost. Argentina could not**. This was a major factor in **the collapse of the Argentine economy** later in the 1980s and the overthrow of the military government.

959. **In 2013, a non-binding vote or "referendum" was taken in the Falklands.** A large majority of the people voted to remain a British territory.

960. **Today, the Falkland Islands remain under British control.** The population has grown significantly since the war ended.

The Good Friday Agreement
(1998)

This chapter will explore the significance of **the Good Friday Agreement and its lasting impact on Northern Ireland**. Let's discover twenty facts about **the agreement and how it was designed to bring peace to the region.** We'll also discover **how the agreement provided for the release of prisoners** and the establishment of human rights acts and organizations.

961. **Northern Ireland remained part of Great Britain when the rest of Ireland won its independence in 1921**. Most of the people in the south were **Catholic**. A significant minority in Northern Ireland were **Protestant**. They were worried their right to worship freely would be taken away if Northern Ireland became part of Ireland.

962. **From the late 1960s to 1998, Northern Ireland went through a period of time called the Troubles. Catholic and Protestant paramilitary groups fought each other** in the streets of Northern Irish cities, especially the biggest city, **Belfast**.

963. **Cities like Belfast had been unofficially divided along religious lines for decades**. During the Troubles, **it was dangerous for a Catholic to be in Protestant areas** and vice versa.

964. **The British Army had a sizable presence in Northern Ireland during the Troubles.** British forces were accused by Catholics of committing many human rights abuses. Though **the British Army's role was to keep the peace**, it often found itself fighting against paramilitary groups and demonstrations that often included women and children.

965. **The Irish Republican Army or "IRA" was the biggest Catholic paramilitary group in Northern Ireland**. As of 2023, its political wing, **Sinn Fein**, is the largest party in the territory.

966. Many **Protestant paramilitaries existed, including the UDF or Ulster Defence Force.**

967. **The Good Friday Agreement was signed in 1998**. The agreement was named after the holiday it fell on, **Good Friday**. This agreement was a **major breakthrough in the history of Northern Ireland.**

968. **The Good Friday Agreement established the North-South Ministerial Council.** This council allowed for cooperation between the governments of Northern Ireland and Southern Ireland.

969. **Northern Ireland was given its own parliament and ministers, allowing for more independence.**

970. **Under the agreement, citizens of Northern Ireland have the right to hold both British and Irish passports,** though not all do.

971. **The Good Friday Agreement brought about the Single Equality Commission**, which aims to promote equality for all citizens.

972. **Guarantees were made regarding the Irish language and cultural rights.**

973. **Paramilitary prisoners were released, and the Police Service of Northern Ireland was created.** The police force was made up of both Catholics and Protestants.

974. **The Northern Ireland Assembly**, which is responsible for making decisions on issues like health care, education, and transport, was created because of this agreement.

975. **The Independent Commission on Policing was another result of the agreement.** The commission was responsible for reforming the police forces of Northern Ireland.

976. **The Good Friday Agreement was also responsible for establishing a new criminal justice system in Northern Ireland.**

977. Thanks to the Good Friday Agreement, **the Human Rights Commission and the Equality Commission were started.**

978. **Peace was further served by instituting the Northern Ireland Executive,** which is responsible for the day-to-day running of the region.

979. **Despite vast improvements, there are still tensions between the two religious groups in Northern Ireland**, particularly during the so-called **"Marching Season."** During this time, conservative and sometimes extremist Protestant groups hold marches through Catholic areas on religious occasions from April to August.

980. **In 2023, new concerns have been brought up by all sides in Northern Ireland over Britain's exit from the European Union.** Many in Northern Ireland fear their economy will suffer. Most people were against Brexit.

Brexit

(2016–2023)

Now we bring ourselves to the present day. **This section will explore Brexit: Britain's decision to exit the European Union.** We will cover **the referendum, negotiations, political unrest, and anti-immigration sentiment** in twenty facts. These events have **had a great impact on the UK's relationship with other countries**, as well as the lives of its citizens. Let's see how.

981. **The EU, or European Union, is an organization of twenty-seven countries** whose economies, monetary policies, and much else are governed **by the European Commission**, the main governing body of the EU.

982. **Brexit is a word that describes the United Kingdom leaving the European Union (EU).** The name **"Brexit"** is a combination of the words **"British" and "exit."**

983. **The Brexit movement began in the 2010s when many British people began to feel that much of their economic and political independence was being lost to the EU.**

984. **More than seventeen million citizens voted to leave the EU on June 23rd, 2016. About sixteen million voted to stay**. These numbers may have changed since 2016, but the UK is still deeply divided over Brexit.

985. **Those voting to leave the EU said they wanted the UK to be more independent.**

986. **UK Prime Minister David Cameron wanted the UK to stay in the EU**. He resigned after losing the vote.

987. **Prime Minister Theresa May officially triggered the Brexit process on March 29th, 2017,** by way of **Article 50 of the Lisbon Treaty**, which cemented many of the rules and policies of the European Union.

988. **A transition period was agreed upon by both entities**, allowing UK businesses to continue trading with the EU until December 2020.

989. **Negotiations between the UK and the EU were difficult and long**, but Britain finally left the EU in 2020.

990. **The UK had to decide how it would trade with the EU and other countries and how it would protect the rights of people from the EU who lived in the UK.**

991. **Some people in the UK are worried that leaving the EU will make it harder for them to travel,** work, and live in other parts of Europe.

992. **The proposed new rules for immigration to Britain included a visa-waiver program for citizens from countries outside the EU.**

993. **The EU created a financial aid package worth €500 million to help farmers and fishermen absorb the losses** they faced if they were unable to trade farm goods easily with **the UK or fish in British waters**.

994. **British companies must now pay extra costs (tariffs) to trade with other European countries**. People in Britain worry that tariffs will cause a significant increase in prices.

995. **The British currency, the pound, suffered a significant loss after the passage of Brexit,** primarily because the UK faced the unknown.

996. **The UK will no longer be part of the European Union's single currency**, which means that the pound will likely be worth less than the euro.

997. **The UK will no longer be part of the European Union's political and economic systems,** which means it will have to find new ways to work together with other European countries. **This could benefit the UK because it will allow the country to set up its own trade agreements** without having to submit them to the EU for approval.

998. **The UK no longer has to follow the same laws as other countries in the EU**.

999. **Brexit could end up costing the UK economy as much as £66 billion every year, though estimates run from £40 billion to £75 billion or more.** This is because of the loss of trade and trade privileges with most of Europe.

1000. **Brexit has been a big issue all over the world**. Many people are watching to see how it all turns out because **it will affect the world economy**.

Conclusion

***Our journey has taken us through centuries of history**. We have explored many events that have **shaped the United Kingdom**. Learning about **England's history** is an important and fascinating endeavor. **From the Norman Conquest to the Industrial Revolution** and beyond, the country has been shaped by a rich and complex set of events, figures, and ideas.*

***Exploring England's past provides invaluable insight into the development of its political, social, and economic systems and its contributions to global culture**. Its stories are rich with the drama and intrigue of human experience. It is no wonder that **so many people are captivated by England's past;** it provides so many interesting topics to study!*

***Thanks for joining us on this amazing, many-faceted trip through England's history**. We hope we have encouraged you to learn more about its history.*

Sources and Additional References

Hines, John. *The Anglo-Saxons from the Migration Period to the Eighth Century: An Ethnographic Perspective*. Boydell and Brewer, 1997.

Stenton, Sir Frank M. *Anglo-Saxon England*. Oxford University Press, 1971.

Barlow, Frank. *The Feudal Kingdom of England 1042-1216*. Routledge, 2002.

Gillingham, John. *The Norman Conquest*. Routledge, 2002.

Bates, David. *William the Conqueror*. Yale University Press, 2009.

Keegan, John. *The Face of Battle*. Viking Press, 1976.

Barron, Caroline M. *The Reign of Edward III: Crown and Political Society in England, 1327-1377*. Yale University Press, 1990.

Bartlett, Robert. *England under the Norman and Angevin Kings, 1075-1225*. Oxford University Press, 2000.

Hindley, Geoffrey. *A Brief History of the Hundred Years War*. Robinson, 2006.

Vaughan, Richard. *The Hundred Years War: The English in France, 1337-1453*. University of California Press, 1999.

Ross, Charles. *The Wars of the Roses*. Thames and Hudson, 1976.

Bainton, Roland H. *The Reformation of the Sixteenth Century*. Beacon Press, 1952.

Wernham, R. B. *The Making of Elizabethan Foreign Policy, 1558-1603*. Stanford University Press, 1980.

Williams, Neville. *Elizabeth I: Queen of England*. Atheneum, 1967.

Adamson, John. *The Civil Wars: A Military History of England, Scotland, and Ireland, 1638-1660* (Oxford University Press, 1998).

Burrow, John A. *History of Histories of the English Civil War* (Cambridge University Press, 2008).

Durston, Gregory. *The Later Stuarts, 1660-1714* (Longman, 1996).

Harris, Tim. Revolution: *The Great Crisis of the British Monarchy, 1685-1720* (Penguin Books, 2006).

Porter, Roy. *The Creation of the Modern World: The Untold Story of the British Enlightenment* (W.W. Norton and Company, 2000).

Goose, Nigel. *The Industrial Revolution* (Routledge, 2005).

Hobsbawm, Eric. *Industry and Empire: An Economic History of Britain Since 1750* (Weidenfeld and Nicolson, 1968).

Palmer, Colin A. *The Slaves of Britain: Blacks in Britain, 1780-1850* (Oxford University Press, 2014).

Walvin, James. *The Slave Trade: The Story of the Atlantic Slave Trade, 1440-1870* (Simon and Schuster, 1997).

Morris, Rose. *The Oxford Illustrated History of the British Monarchy*. Oxford University Press, 1988.

Thompson, R. M. *The War in the Crimea*. Kessinger Publishing, 2007.

Butler, Joseph. *The Great Famine and the Irish Diaspora in America*. University of Massachusetts Press, 1994.

Finnan, Joseph. *The Irish Famine: A Documentary History*. Irish Academic Press, 2009.

Kastner, Jens. *The Great Exhibition of 1851: A Nation on Show*. Bloomsbury Academic, 2014.

Fay, C.R. *The Boer War*. Oxford University Press, 2010.

Horne, John. *The Great War: 1914-1918*. Penguin, 2003.

Prior, Robin. *To Arms: The Great War 1914-1918*. Oxford University Press, 2003.

Jones, Mary. *The British Labour Movement and the General Strike of 1926*. Routledge, 2008.

Rosenberg, Jennifer. "Overview of World War II." ThoughtCo, Aug. 28, 2019, thoughtco.com/world-war-ii-1779792.

Powell, Martin. *The Welfare State in Britain since 1945*. Palgrave Macmillan, 2007.

Bull, Stephen J. *Britain, Egypt, and the Middle East: Imperial Policy in the Aftermath of the Suez Crisis, 1957-1961*. Routledge, 2004.

"Margaret Thatcher (1979–90)." BBC, BBC, www.bbc.co.uk/history/historic_figures/thatcher_margaret.shtml.

"Margaret Thatcher and the 1980s." The British Library, www.bl.uk/20th-century-literature/articles/margaret-thatcher-and-the-1980s.

"Falklands War." Encyclopedia Britannica, www.britannica.com/event/Falklands-War.

"Good Friday Agreement: 20 Years On." The British Library, www.bl.uk/20th-century-literature/articles/good-friday-agreement-20-years-on.

"The Good Friday Agreement: What Is It?" The Guardian, www.theguardian.com/world/2018/mar/19/the-good-friday-agreement-what-is-it.

"Brexit Timeline: How Britain Voted to Leave the EU." BBC, BBC, www.bbc.co.uk/news/uk-politics-32810887.

"Brexit: A Very British Revolution." The British Library, www.bl.uk/20th-century-literature/articles/brexit-a-very-british-revolution.

Welcome Aboard, Check Out This Limited-Time Free Bonus!

Ahoy, reader! Welcome to the Ahoy Publications family, and thanks for snagging a copy of this book! Since you've chosen to join us on this journey, we'd like to offer you something special.

Check out the link below for a FREE e-book filled with delightful facts about American History.

But that's not all - you'll also have access to our exclusive email list with even more free e-books and insider knowledge. Well, what are ye waiting for? Visit the link below to join and set sail toward exciting adventures in American History.

To access your limited-time free bonus, go to: ahoypublications.com/

Made in United States
Orlando, FL
10 July 2024

48794879R00076